MY FINAL ANSWER

BIBLE TRIVIA

THIRTY INTERACTIVE QUIZZES
THAT PUT *YOU* IN THE HOT SEAT

PAUL KENT

BARBOUR
PUBLISHING, INC.
Uhrichsville, Ohio

MY FINAL ANSWER

BIBLE TRIVIA

ISBN 1-58660-030-3

Published by Barbour Publishing, Inc., P. O. Box 719, Uhrichsville, Ohio 44683 http://www.barbourbooks.com

 Member of the
Evangelical Christian
Publishers Association

Printed in the United States of America.

the you will read here that may you had three Bible trivia one thirty carefully, try to measure your your own responses, and see how God stays up with you, or

INTRODUCTION

Here's the Bible trivia book you've been waiting for: *My Final Answer!* Each of these thirty interactive quizzes will test your Scripture knowledge with fun, interesting, and increasingly more difficult questions. Read it yourself, or use it in a group—the book's setup lends itself well to a "quiz show" format, with a contestant and a moderator.

Each quiz features twelve levels of multiple-choice questions, beginning with easy material you might have learned as a kid in Sunday school. But the challenge increases as you move through the levels. Get through four levels without a wrong answer, and you've won Bible Bronze. If you can successfully navigate eight levels of questioning, you'll earn Bible Silver. And if you can complete all twelve levels without a miss, you'll win Bible Gold! Be forewarned, though—you need to know your Bible awfully well to answer those higher-level questions!

But you will have help. In each quiz, you get three Bible Bonuses: Use them carefully (in combination with your Bible knowledge) and you can win! Once in each quiz, you can:

DOUBLE YOUR CHANCES (beginning on page 193): Look up this bonus to learn two of the wrong answers.

HAVE A HINT (beginning on page 205): Look up this bonus to get some extra information—it may be a word play or some reference to the popular culture— to give you a clue to the correct answer.

LOOK IN THE BOOK (beginning on page 229): Look up this bonus for the question's Bible reference...then find your final answer in your final authority.

Remember—you get a total of three Bible Bonuses (one of each) in each twelve-question quiz. And please note that all Bible Bonuses, like the answers, are listed by level rather than by quiz. That way, you won't inadvertently see information on the next question as you're checking out your current one.

The ANSWER section begins on page 241.

One final note: Direct Bible quotations in the questions are taken from the New International Version of the Bible—but they should be general enough for those more familiar with other Bible translations.

So are you ready for the challenge? Step up to the "hot seat" and show us your Bible knowledge! As you prove how much you know, keep in mind James 1:22—the importance of *acting* on what you know. That's what Bible knowledge is all about—and that's *My Final Answer!*

BIBLE
QUIZZES

BIBLE
TRIVIA

THIRTY INTERACTIVE QUIZZES THAT PUT YOU IN THE HOT SEAT

QUIZ 1

LEVEL 1

What was the name of the first man?
- a) Fred
- b) Adam
- c) Noah
- d) John the Baptist

Page 193   Page 205   Page 229   Page 241

LEVEL 2

Which disciple betrayed Jesus for thirty pieces of silver?

a) Andrew
b) Simon the Zealot
c) Judas Iscariot
d) Philip

LEVEL 3

What personal friend did Jesus raise from the dead?

a) Lazarus
b) John
c) Mary
d) Martha

BIBLE BRONZE

According to the apostle Paul, the wages of sin is what?

a) disease
b) pain
c) death
d) grief

Pages 194–196   Pages 207–212   Pages 230–232   Pages 242–244

LEVEL 5

With what woman did King David commit adultery?

a) Bathsheba   c) Delilah
b) Hannah   d) Tamar

LEVEL 6

Isaiah prophesied that Jesus would be "a man of" what?

a) joy   c) power
b) sorrows   d) pain

LEVEL 7

According to the apostle Paul, what "governmental" role do believers play for Christ?

a) tax collectors
b) governors
c) ambassadors
d) commissioners

Pages 197–199   Pages 213–218   Pages 233–235   Pages 245–247

BIBLE SILVER

According to David, how far has God "removed
our transgressions from us"?
   a) as far as the east is from the west
   b) as far as the earth is from the stars
   c) as far as a man can travel
   d) as far as the light can pierce the darkness

LEVEL 9

In the book of John, Jesus said the world would
recognize his disciples by what?
   a) their faith
   b) their good works
   c) their love
   d) their wisdom

LEVEL 10

To whom is the book of Acts addressed?
   a) Theophilus   c) Cornelius
   b) Barnabas   d) Eutychus

Pages 200–202   Pages 219–224   Pages 236–238   Pages 248–250

LEVEL 11

Where did Moses flee to after killing an Egyptian?
- a) Mesopotamia
- b) Megiddo
- c) Mitylene
- d) Midian

BIBLE GOLD

What Old Testament prophet was a shepherd from Tekoa?
- a) Micah
- b) Nahum
- c) Amos
- d) Zechariah

Pages 203–204   Pages 225–228   Pages 239–240   Pages 251–252

BIBLE
TRIVIA

THIRTY INTERACTIVE QUIZZES THAT PUT YOU IN THE HOT SEAT

QUIZ 2

LEVEL 1

Who built an ark to protect his family, seven of every clean animal, and two of every unclean animal from a devastating worldwide flood?

a) Moses
b) Abraham
c) Noah
d) Captain Kangaroo

Page 193   Page 205   Page 229   Page 241

LEVEL 2

How does John 3:16 begin?
- a) "In the beginning God…"
- b) "But those who hope in the Lord…"
- c) "But God demonstrates his own love…"
- d) "For God so loved the world…"

LEVEL 3

What baby, a future Israelite leader, was placed in a basket in the Nile River?
- a) Joseph
- c) David
- b) Moses
- d) Nehemiah

BIBLE BRONZE

What Roman governor allowed the crucifixion of Jesus?
- a) Quirinius
- b) Pilate
- c) Felix
- d) Festus

Pages 194–196   Pages 207–212   Pages 230–232   Pages 242–244

LEVEL 5

According to the apostle Paul, how will the day of Jesus' return come?

- a) like a thief in the night
- b) like a mighty trumpet
- c) like a flash of lightning
- d) like an eagle swooping

LEVEL 6

Who was Jacob's father?

- a) Abraham
- c) Isaac
- b) Lot
- d) Joseph

LEVEL 7

Which of the following is not on the apostle Paul's list of things to think about?

- a) whatever is true
- b) whatever is pure
- c) whatever is lovely
- d) whatever is pleasing

Pages 197–199   Pages 213–218   Pages 233–235   Pages 245–247

BIBLE SILVER

What king's prayer added fifteen years to his life?

- a) David
- b) Hezekiah
- c) Jehoshaphat
- d) Ahaziah

LEVEL 9

After the crucifixion, who asked Pilate for Jesus' body?

- a) Simon of Cyrene
- b) Joseph of Arimathea
- c) Mary of Magdala
- d) Apollos of Alexandria

LEVEL 10

Which of the following is not listed as part of King Nebuchadnezzar's punishment for pride?

- a) He ate grass like cattle.
- b) His hair grew like a bird's feathers.
- c) His nails grew like a bird's claws.
- d) He slept in a wet cave.

Pages 200–202   Pages 219–224   Pages 236–238   Pages 248–250

LEVEL 11

What king died in the year that Isaiah received his commission from the Lord?

- a) Amaziah
- b) Uzziah
- c) Jotham
- d) Ahaz

BIBLE GOLD

Which of these churches of Asia Minor did Jesus threaten to spit from his mouth?

- a) Ephesus
- b) Smyrna
- c) Philadelphia
- d) Laodicea

Pages 203–204 Pages 225–228 Pages 239–240 Pages 251–252

BIBLE TRIVIA

THIRTY INTERACTIVE QUIZZES THAT PUT YOU IN THE HOT SEAT

QUIZ 3

LEVEL 1

Who conquered the warrior Goliath?
a) David
b) Jonathan
c) Malachi
d) Jack the Giant Killer

Page 193

Page 205

Page 229

Page 241

LEVEL 2

What judge of Israel was known for his long hair and great strength?
- a) Tola
- b) Samson
- c) Gideon
- d) Hercules

LEVEL 3

Who cursed the day of his birth after suffering multiple attacks of Satan?
- a) Jacob
- c) Job
- b) Ezekiel
- d) Malachi

BIBLE BRONZE

Who wrote the book of Revelation?
- a) John
- b) James
- c) Jude
- d) Jeremiah

Pages 194–196   Pages 207–212   Pages 230–232   Pages 242–244

LEVEL 5

According to Jesus, it is less likely for a rich man to enter God's kingdom than for a camel to what?

- a) fly
- b) go through the eye of a needle
- c) speak
- d) have triplets

LEVEL 6

According to the book of 1 Timothy, what is a "root of all kinds of evil"?

- a) pride
- b) sex
- c) Satan
- d) the love of money

LEVEL 7

On which mountain did Noah's ark settle as the great flood subsided?

- a) Ararat
- b) Hermon
- c) Moriah
- d) Nebo

Pages 197–199 Pages 213–218 Pages 233–235 Pages 245–247

BIBLE SILVER

Which of the following was not one of Satan's temptations of Christ?

    a) changing stones into bread
    b) jumping off the temple
    c) worshiping the devil
    d) striking the wicked with blindness

LEVEL 9

"Golgotha," the site of Jesus' crucifixion, means what?

    a) The Hill of Sorrows
    b) The Potter's Field
    c) The Place of the Skull
    d) The Well of the Oath

LEVEL 10

Who deserted Paul and Barnabas, and their missionary work, in Pamphylia?

    a) Silas   c) Judas Barsabbas
    b) John Mark   d) Linus

Pages 200–202   Pages 219–224   Pages 236–238   Pages 248–250

LEVEL 11

Which of the following is not a part of the famous "a time for everything" passage in Ecclesiastes?

a) a time to be born and a time to die
b) a time to sleep and a time to wake
c) a time to weep and a time to laugh
d) a time to love and a time to hate

BIBLE GOLD

What was the name of the man who had an ear cut off, and healed, during Christ's arrest?

a) Malchus
b) Zenas
c) Aristarchus
d) Archippus

Pages 203–204   Pages 225–228   Pages 239–240   Pages 251–252

BIBLE TRIVIA

THIRTY INTERACTIVE QUIZZES THAT PUT YOU IN THE HOT SEAT

QUIZ 4

LEVEL 1

What was the name of Jesus' mother?
   a) Ruth
   b) Esther
   c) Martha
   d) Mary

Page 193

Page 205

Page 229

Page 241

LEVEL 2

How does the famous 23rd Psalm begin?
- a) "The earth is the Lord's…"
- b) "The Lord is my shepherd…"
- c) "Blessed is the man…"
- d) "Great is the Lord…"

LEVEL 3

Before his conversion, what was the apostle Paul's name?
- a) Simon
- b) Elymas
- c) Saul
- d) Moses

BIBLE BRONZE

Who committed the first murder?
- a) Adam
- b) Cain
- c) Abel
- d) Lamech

Pages 194–196   Pages 207–212   Pages 230–232   Pages 242–244

LEVEL 5

Which disciple demanded to see the nail prints in Jesus' hands and feet before he would believe in the Resurrection?

   a) Bartholomew   c) Simon the Zealot

   b) James   d) Thomas

LEVEL 6

According to the apostle Paul, what kind of giver does God love?

   a) cheerful   c) prompt

   b) generous   d) regular

LEVEL 7

Which of the following is not among the names of Christ in Isaiah's prophecy?

   a) Mighty God

   b) Everlasting Father

   c) Prince of Peace

   d) Hope of Man

Pages 197–199 Pages 213–218 Pages 233–235 Pages 245–247

BIBLE SILVER

What woman, known for her good works, did Peter raise from the dead in Joppa?

a) Tabitha
b) Lydia
c) Drusilla
d) Bernice

LEVEL 9

Which of the following did not appear at the Transfiguration?

a) Jesus
b) Moses
c) Elijah
d) Samuel

LEVEL 10

Who helped carry Jesus' cross to Golgotha?

a) Micah of Moresheth
b) Simon of Cyrene
c) Joseph of Arimathea
d) Joseph of Cyprus

Pages 200–202   Pages 219–224   Pages 236–238   Pages 248–250

LEVEL 11

Who died after touching the Ark of the Covenant?
- a) Uzzah
- b) Mahlon
- c) Ahio
- d) Naphtali

BIBLE GOLD

Sanballat and Tobiah are villains in what biblical book?
- a) Esther
- b) Nehemiah
- c) Obadiah
- d) Daniel

Pages 203–204   Pages 225–228   Pages 239–240   Pages 251–252

BIBLE TRIVIA

THIRTY INTERACTIVE QUIZZES THAT PUT YOU IN THE HOT SEAT

QUIZ 5

LEVEL 1

What set of rules did God give to Moses?
- a) the Four Spiritual Laws
- b) the Seven Habits of Highly Successful
  People
- c) the Ten Commandments
- d) the Twelve-Step Program

Page 193

Page 205

Page 229

Page 241

LEVEL 2

According to the book of Revelation, the streets of the New Jerusalem are made of what?

- a) gold
- b) silver
- c) cedar
- d) asphalt

LEVEL 3

According to Psalm 119, God's Word is a lamp to what?

- a) my feet
- b) the darkness
- c) His people
- d) the blind

BIBLE BRONZE

What did the apostle Paul call the ninefold characteristics (love, joy, peace, etc.) of the maturing Christian?

- a) the harvest of faith
- b) the works of the righteous
- c) the fruit of the Spirit
- d) the life of Christ

LEVEL 5

How did Judas Iscariot kill himself after betraying Jesus?
- a) by hanging
- b) by drinking poison
- c) by jumping off a cliff
- d) by drowning

LEVEL 6

Who had a donkey that spoke?
- a) Ahab
- c) Solomon
- b) Jehoshaphat
- d) Balaam

LEVEL 7

What is the more commonly-known name of the Bible character Hadassah?
- a) Abraham
- b) Esther
- c) Gideon
- d) Mary Magdalene

Pages 197–199   Pages 213–218   Pages 233–235   Pages 245–247

BIBLE SILVER

According to the apostle Paul, what never fails?
- a) love
- b) truth
- c) faith
- d) God

LEVEL 9

According to the book of Hebrews, Jesus is a high priest in the order of whom?
- a) Aaron
- b) Joshua
- c) Eleazar
- d) Melchizedek

LEVEL 10

Who was known as a "mighty hunter before the Lord"?
- a) David
- b) Gideon
- c) Nimrod
- d) Ishmael

Pages 200–202   Pages 219–224   Pages 236–238   Pages 248–250

LEVEL 11

What was the name of the servant girl who met Peter after an angel freed him from prison?

a) Lydia

c) Rhoda

b) Euodia

d) Priscilla

BIBLE GOLD

Which of the following is not a physical compliment from the Song of Solomon?

a) "Your nose is like the tower of Lebanon."

b) "Your navel is a rounded goblet."

c) "Your fingers are like limbs of cedar."

d) "Your eyes are the pools of Heshbon."

Pages 203–204   Pages 225–228   Pages 239–240   Pages 251–252

BIBLE TRIVIA

THIRTY INTERACTIVE QUIZZES THAT PUT YOU IN THE HOT SEAT

QUIZ 6

LEVEL 1

What did Adam name his wife?
- a) Eve
- b) Sarah
- c) Rachel
- d) Honey

Page 193   Page 205   Page 229   Page 241

LEVEL 2

What was the vocation of Jesus' earthly father, Joseph?

- a) priest
- b) shepherd
- c) carpenter
- d) farmer

LEVEL 3

Which of the following is not one of the Ten Commandments?

- a) You shall not murder.
- b) You shall not steal.
- c) Honor your father and mother.
- d) You shall not gossip.

BIBLE BRONZE

Which of the following is not a "fruit of the Spirit"?

- a) love
- b) health
- c) peace
- d) goodness

Pages 194–196   Pages 207–212   Pages 230–232   Pages 242–244

LEVEL 5

What was the apostle Paul's hometown?
- a) Jerusalem
- b) Joppa
- c) Tarsus
- d) Antioch

LEVEL 6

According to Jesus, "the greatest among you will be…"
- a) "the winner of souls."
- b) "the worker of miracles."
- c) "your teacher."
- d) "your servant."

LEVEL 7

What man was struck dead for lying about the amount of money he gave to God?
- a) Silas
- b) Bartimaeus
- c) Ananias
- d) Nicolas

Pages 197–199   Pages 213–218   Pages 233–235   Pages 245–247

BIBLE SILVER

What group of people was commended for comparing Paul's teachings with the Scriptures?

a) the Thessalonians   c) the Colossians
b) the Bereans   d) the Galatians

LEVEL 9

In a vision of Isaiah, what were the seraphs over the Lord's throne calling one to another?

a) "Holy, holy, holy"
b) "The Lord God omnipotent reigneth"
c) "Glory to God in the highest"
d) "Praise the Lord"

LEVEL 10

What character in the story of Esther was hanged on a gallows that he had ordered built?

a) Mordecai   c) Haman
b) Xerxes   d) Harbona

Pages 200–202 Pages 219–224 Pages 236–238 Pages 248–250

LEVEL 11

Which of the following is not listed as a source
for the book of Proverbs?

- a) Job
- b) Solomon
- c) King Lemuel
- d) Agur

BIBLE GOLD

Who wrote down the book of Romans for the
apostle Paul?

- a) Lucius
- b) Jason
- c) Tertius
- d) Erastus

Pages 203–204   Pages 225–228   Pages 239–240   Pages 251–252

BIBLE TRIVIA

THIRTY INTERACTIVE QUIZZES THAT PUT YOU IN THE HOT SEAT

QUIZ 7

LEVEL 1

What prophet spent three nights in a fish's stomach?

a) Obadiah
b) Joel
c) Jonah
d) Micah

Page 193

Page 205

Page 229

Page 241

LEVEL 2

According to the psalmist, God owns what on a thousand hills?

- a) the cellular phone towers
- b) the cattle
- c) the dwellings
- d) the oak trees

LEVEL 3

From what miraculous thing did Moses receive his call to leadership?

- a) a staff that became a snake
- b) a burning bush
- c) a rock that gushed forth water
- d) a healed leper

BIBLE BRONZE

Which of the following was not a son of Noah?

- a) Ham
- b) Japheth
- c) Kenan
- d) Shem

Pages 194–196   Pages 207–212   Pages 230–232   Pages 242–244

LEVEL 5

In what town did Jesus spend his youth?
- a) Jerusalem
- b) Nazareth
- c) Bethlehem
- d) Tyre

LEVEL 6

What prophet was taken to heaven in a whirlwind?
- a) Elijah
- c) Samuel
- b) Obadiah
- d) Zephaniah

LEVEL 7

What kept Paul from becoming conceited over his special vision of heaven?
- a) a thorn in the flesh
- b) his partnership with Timothy
- c) the deacons of the church of Corinth
- d) his discipline of service

Pages 197–199 Pages 213–218 Pages 233–235 Pages 245–247

BIBLE SILVER

What title did God tell Moses to use when answering the Israelites' question, "What is his [God's] name?"

- a) Jehovah
- b) Yahweh
- c) I AM
- d) The Lord of Hosts

LEVEL 9

Whom did Eve say "replaced" the murdered Abel?

- a) Seth
- b) Enosh
- c) Jared
- d) Lamech

LEVEL 10

What was the apostle Paul's rule toward people who refused to work?

- a) They should be prayed over.
- b) They should not eat.
- c) They should be disciplined by the church.
- d) They should not expect charity.

Pages 200–202   Pages 219–224   Pages 236–238   Pages 248–250

LEVEL 11

How many siblings, the natural children of Mary and Joseph, did Jesus have?

a) none
c) four
b) two
d) six or more

BIBLE GOLD

According to the Proverbs, what is true of an adulterous woman's speech?

a) It is smoother than oil.
b) It has ensnared many young men.
c) It is full of lies.
d) It can confuse the wise.

Pages 203–204 Pages 225–228 Pages 239–240 Pages 251–252

THIRTY INTERACTIVE QUIZZES THAT PUT YOU IN THE HOT SEAT

BIBLE TRIVIA

QUIZ 8

What new name did God give Abram?
a) Abraham
b) Abel
c) Adam
d) Apple of My Eye

Page 193

Page 205

Page 229

Page 241

LEVEL 2

Which disciple disowned Jesus three times the night of Christ's arrest?

    a) Andrew
    b) James
    c) Philip
    d) Peter

LEVEL 3

What was the name of Moses' brother?

    a) Abraham   c) Aaron
    b) Zipporah   d) Zebulun

BIBLE BRONZE

Where does God keep a record of the names of the saved?

    a) the book of heaven
    b) the book of life
    c) the book of the blessed
    d) the book of the kingdom

Pages 194–196   Pages 207–212   Pages 230–232   Pages 242–244

LEVEL 5

According to Jesus, what belongs to the "poor in spirit"?

a) the joy of the Lord
b) the kingdom of heaven
c) the water of life
d) the wisdom of Solomon

LEVEL 6

Of the twelve men who spied in Canaan, how many believed the Israelites should go in to possess the land?

a) twelve　　　c) two
b) eight　　　d) none

LEVEL 7

Who "walked with God; then he was no more, because God took him away"?

a) Methuselah　　　c) Benjamin
b) Enoch　　　d) Caleb

Pages 197–199 Pages 213–218 Pages 233–235 Pages 245–247

BIBLE SILVER

What miraculous thing did Elisha make an axe head do?

- a) speak
- b) turn to gold
- c) float
- d) heal lepers

LEVEL 9

What did some mockers say of the disciples who spoke in other tongues during Pentecost?

- a) "They are possessed by devils."
- b) "They are only pretending."
- c) "They have had too much wine."
- d) "They have lost their minds."

LEVEL 10

What miraculous event accompanied Joshua's military victory over the Amorites?

- a) His dead soldiers returned to life.
- b) The earth swallowed his enemies.
- c) An angel struck his opponents blind.
- d) The sun stood still for a day.

Pages 200-202   Pages 219-224   Pages 236-238   Pages 248-250

LEVEL 11

Job was from the land of what?

a) Uz   c) Ur

b) On   d) Og

BIBLE GOLD

Which of the following groups of stars is mentioned in Scripture?

a) Gemini

b) Pleiades

c) Perseus

d) Cassiopeia

Pages 203–204   Pages 225–228   Pages 239–240   Pages 251–252

THIRTY INTERACTIVE QUIZZES THAT PUT YOU IN THE HOT SEAT

BIBLE TRIVIA

QUIZ 9

LEVEL 1

Which of the following was not one of Jesus' original disciples?

   a) Peter
   b) John
   c) Moses
   d) Matthew

Page 193

Page 205

Page 229

Page 241

LEVEL 2

What was Adam and Eve's original home?

a) the Garden of Eden
b) the Plains of Moab
c) the Valley of Jericho
d) the Big Apple

LEVEL 3

What man in David's life "loved him as himself"?

a) Saul
b) Joab
c) Abner
d) Jonathan

BIBLE BRONZE

Where did God confuse the language of the early humans?

a) Babel
b) Sodom
c) Gomorrah
d) Nineveh

Pages 194–196   Pages 207–212   Pages 230–232   Pages 242–244

LEVEL 5

According to the psalmist, what do the heavens declare?

   a) the glory of God
   b) the wonders of creation
   c) the beauty of holiness
   d) the strength of the Lord

LEVEL 6

What symbolic action did Pontius Pilate take to argue his own innocence in the crucifixion of Jesus?

   a) He put on a blindfold.
   b) He turned his back on the crowd.
   c) He released a dove.
   d) He washed his hands.

Pages 197–198   Pages 213–216   Pages 233–234   Pages 245–246

LEVEL 7

The apostle Paul warned Christians about being "yoked" with what?

- a) debt
- b) unbelievers
- c) sin
- d) worldly wisdom

BIBLE SILVER

What was the nationality of the giant warrior Goliath?

- a) Philistine
- b) Moabite
- c) Phoenician
- d) Ammonite

LEVEL 9

Why did Peter rebuke a new convert formerly known as "Simon the sorcerer"?

- a) for returning to his sorcery
- b) for calling down curses on Pharisees
- c) for casting out demons without permission
- d) for trying to buy the gift of the Holy Spirit

Pages 199–201   Pages 217–222   Pages 235–237   Pages 247–249

LEVEL 10

What vocation did the apostle Paul have in addition to his missionary work?

a) carpentry
b) fishing
c) tentmaking
d) vinedressing

LEVEL 11

Why did the residents of Malta think the apostle Paul was a god?

a) He raised someone from the dead.
b) A snake bite didn't kill him.
c) He predicted a terrible storm.
d) Angels appeared to strengthen him.

BIBLE GOLD

What idol fell to the ground and broke after the Ark of the Covenant was placed nearby?

a) Dagon
b) Ashtaroth
c) Molech
d) Chemosh

Pages 202–204   Pages 223–228   Pages 238–240   Pages 250–252

BIBLE TRIVIA

THIRTY INTERACTIVE QUIZZES THAT PUT YOU IN THE HOT SEAT

QUIZ 10

LEVEL 1

What punishment did Shadrach, Meschach, and Abednego receive for refusing to worship a golden image?

    a) the lions' den
    b) the fiery furnace
    c) the gallows
    d) the bagpipes

Page 193   Page 205   Page 229   Page 241

LEVEL 2

According to the book of Romans, who has sinned and fallen short of God's glory?

- a) Jews
- b) Gentiles
- c) pagans
- d) all

LEVEL 3

Jesus said, "I am the vine, you are the" what?

- a) grapes
- b) leaves
- c) branches
- d) thorns

BIBLE BRONZE

Who was specially commissioned as Moses' successor as leader of Israel?

- a) Aaron
- b) Joshua
- c) Eli
- d) Nehemiah

Pages 194–196   Pages 207–212   Pages 230–232   Pages 242–244

LEVEL 5

In the "armor of God," what does the shield represent?

a) salvation   c) faith

b) righteousness   d) truth

LEVEL 6

According to the apostle Paul, how are husbands supposed to love their wives?

a) as Abraham cared for Sarah

b) as Christ loved the church

c) as the Spirit gives them power

d) as the hen protects her chicks

Pages 197–198   Pages 213–216   Pages 233–234   Pages 245–246

LEVEL 7

The "potter's field," purchased with the money Judas Iscariot received for betraying Christ, was also known as what?

a) the Field of Blood
b) the Field of Sorrows
c) the Field of Agony
d) the Betrayer's Field

BIBLE SILVER

According to the apostle Paul, godliness with what is "great gain"?

a) peace
b) love
c) contentment
d) friendship

LEVEL 9

What Old Testament book was the Ethiopian eunuch reading when Philip led him to Christ?

a) Psalms
b) Proverbs
c) Isaiah
d) Jeremiah

Pages 199–201   Pages 217–222   Pages 235–237   Pages 247–249

LEVEL 10

Which disciple was the first to enter Jesus' empty tomb?

- a) John
- b) Peter
- c) Matthew
- d) Thomas

LEVEL 11

As a tribute to Jonathan, what descendant of Saul ate at King David's table?

- a) Malki-Shua
- b) Melech
- c) Micah
- d) Mephibosheth

BIBLE GOLD

According to the Proverbs, a prostitute reduces a man to what?

- a) a brute beast
- b) a blind beggar
- c) a blemished bull
- d) a bite of bread

Quiz 11

Level 1

What did God do on the seventh day of the creation week?

- a) He created man.
- b) He created light.
- c) He created music.
- d) He rested.

Page 193   Page 205   Page 229   Page 241

LEVEL 2

What sign sealed God's promise never again to destroy the earth by a flood?

a) the rainbow
b) the bronze serpent
c) the pillar of fire
d) the man in the moon

LEVEL 3

What did Peter notice immediately after his third denial of Christ—just as Jesus had predicted?

a) a shooting star   c) a peal of thunder
b) a mourner's wail   d) a rooster crowing

BIBLE BRONZE

What special test did God give Abraham?

a) to sacrifice his son Isaac
b) to fast forty days in the desert
c) to kill one thousand Philistines
d) to give all he owned to the poor

Pages 194–196 Pages 207–212 Pages 230–232 Pages 242–244

LEVEL 5

On which mountain did Moses receive the Ten Commandments?
- a) Mount Carmel
- b) Mount Nebo
- c) Mount Gilboa
- d) Mount Sinai

LEVEL 6

What advice did Job's wife have for her suffering husband?
- a) "Sacrifice a burnt offering."
- b) "Accept your lot from God."
- c) "Curse God and die."
- d) "Renounce your sin."

LEVEL 7

According to the apostle Paul, "it is better to marry than to" what?
- a) taste the riches of this world
- b) speak in tongues
- c) burn with passion
- d) serve the Lord alone

Pages 197–199   Pages 213–218   Pages 233–235   Pages 245–247

BIBLE SILVER

According to James, what can no man tame?
- a) the lion
- b) the eyes
- c) the devil
- d) the tongue

LEVEL 9

What was Nehemiah's role in the service of King Artaxerxes?
- a) royal historian
- b) baker
- c) cupbearer
- d) military commander

LEVEL 10

In which city did Paul preach about the "unknown god" to the local philosophers?
- a) Athens
- b) Berea
- c) Corinth
- d) Derbe

Pages 200–202   Pages 219–224   Pages 236–238   Pages 248–250

LEVEL 11

What is the better-known name of Belteshazzar?
- a) Aaron
- b) Daniel
- c) Ezekiel
- d) Moses

BIBLE GOLD

What judge of Israel had thirty sons who rode thirty donkeys?
- a) Tola
- b) Jair
- c) Jephthah
- d) Eli

Pages 203–204   Pages 225–228   Pages 239–240   Pages 251–252

BIBLE TRIVIA

THIRTY INTERACTIVE QUIZZES THAT PUT YOU IN THE HOT SEAT

QUIZ 12

LEVEL 1

How many apostles did Jesus personally select?
  a) two
  b) twelve
  c) fifty
  d) one thousand

Page 193   Page 205   Page 229   Page 241

LEVEL 2

On what "twin cities" did God rain fire and brimstone?

a) Minneapolis and St. Paul
b) Tyre and Sidon
c) Sodom and Gomorrah
d) Athens and Corinth

LEVEL 3

Who tested the Lord's will with a fleece?

a) David
b) Gideon
c) Obadiah
d) Lot

BIBLE BRONZE

In their very first meeting, what did Jesus say He would make of Peter and Andrew?

a) workers of miracles
b) servants of God
c) teachers of rabbis
d) fishers of men

Pages 194–196   Pages 207–212   Pages 230–232   Pages 242–244

LEVEL 5

What queen, upon visiting Solomon, raved that "not even half" of his wisdom and achievements had been told to her?

- a) the queen of Sheba
- b) Queen Esther
- c) Queen Jezebel
- d) Queen Athaliah

LEVEL 6

According to the Proverbs, what are we not to "lean on"?

- a) a crooked staff
- b) our own understanding
- c) a double-minded man
- d) the riches of this world

LEVEL 7

What phrase from the book of Genesis describes the marriage of a man and a woman?

- a) one flesh
- b) holy union
- c) children of God
- d) great reward

Pages 197–199   Pages 213–218   Pages 233–235   Pages 245–247

BIBLE SILVER

According to the Proverbs, a good name is what?
- a) better than great riches
- b) difficult to maintain
- c) the heritage of the Lord's children
- d) its own reward

LEVEL 9

Which of David's wives was a daughter of King Saul?
- a) Michal
- b) Abigail
- c) Bathsheba
- d) Ahinoam

LEVEL 10

What vision convinced Peter to share the gospel with the Gentiles?
- a) a man of Macedonia
- b) the third heaven
- c) animals in a sheet
- d) angels on a ladder

LEVEL 11

Who discovered a Jewish plot to kill the apostle
Paul?

a) Paul's nephew
b) Timothy
c) Silas
d) Barnabas

BIBLE GOLD

According to Jude, what did the devil and
Michael the archangel fight over?

a) the conversion of Saul
b) the temptation of Jesus
c) the mind of Judas Iscariot
d) the body of Moses

Pages 203–204   Pages 225–228   Pages 239–240   Pages 251–252

BIBLE TRIVIA

THIRTY INTERACTIVE QUIZZES THAT PUT YOU IN THE HOT SEAT

QUIZ 13

Who climbed a sycamore tree to see Jesus?
   a) Zacchaeus
   b) Nicodemus
   c) Lazarus
   d) Curious George

Page 193

Page 205

Page 229

Page 241

LEVEL 2

Which of the following rivers was not a branch of the river that watered the Garden of Eden?

- a) Gihon
- b) Tigris
- c) Euphrates
- d) Danube

LEVEL 3

Which of the following was a missionary companion of the apostle Paul?

- a) Barnabas
- b) Barbados
- c) Bar-Jesus
- d) Barabbas

BIBLE BRONZE

What is the first of the Ten Commandments?

- a) You shall not murder.
- b) You shall not commit adultery.
- c) You shall have no other gods before me.
- d) Honor your father and your mother.

Pages 194–196   Pages 207–212   Pages 230–232   Pages 242–244

LEVEL 5

What sign protected Israelite homes in Egypt from the plague on the firstborn?

- a) a candle in the window
- b) bread in the oven
- c) a goat in the yard
- d) blood on the doorposts

LEVEL 6

According to Jesus, what would not fall to the ground apart from God's will?

- a) a sparrow
- b) a rain drop
- c) a leaf
- d) brimstone

LEVEL 7

Which biblical man had the longest recorded lifespan?

- a) Adam
- b) Isaac
- c) Methuselah
- d) Noah

Pages 197–199   Pages 213–218   Pages 233–235   Pages 245–247

BIBLE SILVER

Which of the following disciples was not with Jesus when he was arrested at Gethsemane?

- a) Andrew
- b) Peter
- c) James
- d) John

LEVEL 9

Which tribe was in charge of assembling, disassembling, and moving the tabernacle?

- a) the tribe of Reuben
- b) the tribe of Dan
- c) the tribe of Levi
- d) the tribe of Judah

LEVEL 10

What destroyed the golden-headed statue in King Nebuchadnezzar's dream?

- a) a violent whirlwind
- b) a flood of the Euphrates River
- c) a mighty angel of God
- d) a rock not cut by human hands

Pages 200–202 Pages 219–224 Pages 236–238 Pages 248–250

LEVEL 11

In what city did followers of the false goddess Artemis (Diana) riot after Paul's preaching?

a) Ephesus
b) Corinth
c) Rome
d) Philippi

BIBLE GOLD

The book of Nahum prophesies the fall of what city?

a) Babylon
b) Tyre
c) Susa
d) Nineveh

Pages 203–204   Pages 225–228   Pages 239–240   Pages 251–252

BIBLE TRIVIA

THIRTY INTERACTIVE QUIZZES THAT PUT YOU IN THE HOT SEAT

QUIZ 14

What example did Jesus use to define the word "neighbor"?

- a) the good American
- b) the good Egyptian
- c) the good Samaritan
- d) the good Philistine

Page 193

Page 205

Page 229

Page 241

LEVEL 2

What did David use to battle Goliath?
- a) a bazooka
- b) a bow and arrow
- c) a slingshot
- d) a spear

LEVEL 3

What prophet saw a "wheel in the middle of a wheel"?
- a) Ezekiel
- b) Daniel
- c) Haggai
- d) Zechariah

BIBLE BRONZE

According to the book of Revelation, what is the number of "The Beast"?
- a) 13
- c) 666
- b) 57
- d) 1,000

Pages 194–196   Pages 207–212   Pages 230–232   Pages 242–244

LEVEL 5

According to the apostle John, "God is" what?

- a) power
- b) love
- c) wisdom
- d) grace

LEVEL 6

How long did Jesus fast before His temptation by Satan?

- a) three days
- b) a week
- c) three weeks
- d) forty days

LEVEL 7

According to the apostle John, the traitor Judas Iscariot was also what?

- a) an adulterer
- b) a liar
- c) a thief
- d) a murderer

Pages 197–199   Pages 213–218   Pages 233–235   Pages 245–247

BIBLE SILVER

How did Jesus describe his "yoke"?
- a) comfortable
- b) loose
- c) easy
- d) pleasant

LEVEL 9

According to Jesus, where is a prophet "without honor"?
- a) in the synagogue
- b) in his own house
- c) in Samaria
- d) in this world

LEVEL 10

What did Paul suggest Timothy should take for his frequent illnesses?
- a) wine
- b) cheese
- c) honey
- d) herbs

Pages 200–202   Pages 219–224   Pages 236–238   Pages 248–250

LEVEL 11

What did a seraph touch to Isaiah's lips to take away his guilt and sin?

    a) a golden bowl
    b) a budding pole
    c) a live coal
    d) a sealed scroll

BIBLE GOLD

Which famous Bible character shared his name with a lesser-known biblical woman?

    a) Adam
    b) Daniel
    c) Moses
    d) Noah

Pages 203–204 Pages 225–228 Pages 239–240 Pages 251–252

BIBLE
TRIVIA

· THIRTY INTERACTIVE QUIZZES THAT PUT YOU IN THE HOT SEAT ·

QUIZ 15

What Old Testament character received a "coat of many colors" from his doting father?

a) Adam
b) Joseph
c) Job
d) Goliath

Page 193

Page 205

Page 229

Page 241

LEVEL 2

Who was crucified with Jesus?
- a) Peter
- b) two robbers
- c) a murderer
- d) two insurrectionists

LEVEL 3

Which of the following siblings does the Bible identify as twins?
- a) Moses and Aaron
- b) Jacob and Esau
- c) Peter and Andrew
- d) Mary and Martha

BIBLE BRONZE

The apostle Paul compared the Christian life to what sporting event?
- a) a wrestling match
- b) a race
- c) weight lifting
- d) gymnastics

Pages 194–196　Pages 207–212　Pages 230–232　Pages 242–244

LEVEL 5

What was Cain's flippant response when God asked him where Abel was?

- a) "Why would I care?"
- b) "Find him yourself."
- c) "I don't know anyone named Abel."
- d) "Am I my brother's keeper?"

LEVEL 6

How many wives did King Solomon have?

- a) one
- b) thirty
- c) one hundred
- d) seven hundred

LEVEL 7

How did the sign on Jesus' cross describe Him?

- a) "Traitor to Rome"
- b) "The King of the Jews"
- c) "The Blasphemer"
- d) "Son of a Virgin"

Pages 197–199   Pages 213–218   Pages 233–235   Pages 245–247

BIBLE SILVER

What is the name of the fourth horseman in the book of Revelation?

- a) Pestilence
- b) Death
- c) War
- d) Famine

LEVEL 9

What was Jesus discussing when he mentioned the name of Caesar?

- a) the fall of Rome
- b) idolatry
- c) paying taxes
- d) unjust leadership

LEVEL 10

According to James, what is "friendship with the world"?

- a) a grievous sin
- b) hatred toward God
- c) a poisonous viper
- d) the foolishness of man

Pages 200–202   Pages 219–224   Pages 236–238   Pages 248–250

LEVEL 11

Whose spirit did King Saul seek when consulting with the witch of Endor?

a) Moses'
b) Joshua's
c) Eli's
d) Samuel's

BIBLE GOLD

Which of the following does the Bible not list as a gate in the wall of Jerusalem?

a) Valley Gate
b) Dung Gate
c) Lion Gate
d) Fountain Gate

Pages 203–204 Pages 225–228 Pages 239–240 Pages 251–252

THIRTY INTERACTIVE QUIZZES THAT PUT YOU IN THE HOT SEAT

BIBLE TRIVIA

QUIZ 16

LEVEL 1

In what town was Jesus born?

- a) Bethlehem
- b) Ephesus
- c) Rome
- d) Philadelphia

Page 193   Page 205   Page 229   Page 241

LEVEL 2

What woman led to Samson's downfall?
- a) Herodias
- b) Jezebel
- c) Delilah
- d) Tokyo Rose

LEVEL 3

According to John, what was "in the beginning"?
- a) nothing
- b) the heavens and the earth
- c) the Spirit
- d) the Word

BIBLE BRONZE

In response to God's offer, what one thing did Solomon request?
- a) wealth
- c) wisdom
- b) honor
- d) long life

Pages 194–196   Pages 207–212   Pages 230–232   Pages 242–244

LEVEL 5

According to Jeremiah, where does one go to find balm?

a) Babylon
b) Jerusalem
c) Gilead
d) Beersheba

LEVEL 6

In the "Triumphal Entry," how did Jesus enter Jerusalem?

a) on foot
b) on a white horse
c) on a donkey
d) in a golden chariot

LEVEL 7

Which son of David was known for his exceptional good looks?

a) Amnon
b) Absalom
c) Adonijah
d) Ithream

Pages 197–199   Pages 213–218   Pages 233–235   Pages 245–247

BIBLE SILVER

Who wove the crown of thorns that Jesus wore?
- a) Pontius Pilate
- b) Caiaphas, the high priest
- c) Herod
- d) Roman soldiers

LEVEL 9

According to the Proverbs, what has the power of life and death?
- a) the tongue
- b) the king
- c) the rich
- d) the heart

LEVEL 10

Who initially resisted Elijah's suggestion that he wash seven times in the Jordan River to cure his leprosy?
- a) Ben-Hadad
- b) Gehazi
- c) Naaman
- d) Zedekiah

Pages 200–202   Pages 219–224   Pages 236–238   Pages 248–250

LEVEL 11

Which disciple was so well known for his healing powers that people hoped to be touched by his shadow?

a) Paul
b) Philip
c) Peter
d) Stephen

BIBLE GOLD

Who was the well-known brother of Lahmi?

a) King Saul
b) Goliath
c) Gideon
d) Nebuchadnezzar

Pages 203–204   Pages 225–228   Pages 239–240   Pages 251–252

THIRTY INTERACTIVE QUIZZES THAT PUT YOU IN THE HOT SEAT

BIBLE TRIVIA

QUIZ 17

LEVEL 1

What led the wise men to the baby Jesus?

   a) a billboard
   b) a dove
   c) a cloud
   d) a star

Page 193   Page 205   Page 229   Page 241

LEVEL 2

Which of the following was Abraham's wife?

- a) Mary Lincoln
- b) Sarah
- c) Rebekah
- d) Rachel

LEVEL 3

In the Lord's Prayer, which phrase immediately follows "Our Father in heaven"?

- a) "Give us today our daily bread"
- b) "Lead us not into temptation"
- c) "Hallowed be your name"
- d) "Forgive us our debts"

BIBLE BRONZE

What do the righteous (or just) live by?

- a) faith
- b) godly power
- c) truth
- d) the Spirit's strength

Pages 194–196   Pages 207–212   Pages 230–232   Pages 242–244

LEVEL 5

The Word of God is sharper than what?
 a) a spear
 b) a double-edged sword
 c) a needle
 d) a polished flint

LEVEL 6

Which one of the following animals were Israelites permitted to eat?
 a) pig
 b) camel
 c) cow
 d) rabbit

LEVEL 7

What did Paul tell Christians to "set your minds [or affection] on"?
 a) things above
 b) the Scriptures
 c) prayer
 d) holiness

Pages 197–199 Pages 213–218 Pages 233–235 Pages 245–247

BIBLE SILVER

Where did Jesus say His followers would never walk?

- a) in sin
- b) in sorrow
- c) in darkness
- d) in fear

LEVEL 9

Where were two of Christ's followers going when the resurrected Jesus joined them on the road?

- a) Emmaus
- b) Jerusalem
- c) Samaria
- d) Rome

LEVEL 10

How did the Roman soldiers hasten the deaths of the robbers crucified with Jesus?

- a) by giving them poison
- b) by cutting off their heads
- c) by spearing them
- d) by breaking their legs

Pages 200–202   Pages 219–224   Pages 236–238   Pages 248–250

LEVEL 11

Which of the following precious stones is not part of the New Jerusalem's foundation?

a) diamond
b) sapphire
c) emerald
d) amethyst

BIBLE GOLD

By what other name was the apostle Thomas known?

a) Didymus
b) Bithynia
c) Tychicus
d) Aenon

Pages 203–204   Pages 225–228   Pages 239–240   Pages 251–252

BIBLE TRIVIA

THIRTY INTERACTIVE QUIZZES THAT PUT YOU IN THE HOT SEAT

QUIZ 18

Where did Mary and Joseph place the newborn baby Jesus?

   a) in a basket
   b) in a crib
   c) in a manger
   d) on a sheep

Page 193

Page 205

Page 229

Page 241

LEVEL 2

What was "manna"?
- a) an Israelite rock band
- b) a disease
- c) a type of food
- d) a sacred scroll

LEVEL 3

What animal did Aaron fashion a golden idol to represent?
- a) a calf
- b) an eagle
- c) a snake
- d) a lion

BIBLE BRONZE

Which of the following statements did Jesus make just before He died on the cross?
- a) "It is painful."
- b) "It is unfair."
- c) "It is finished."
- d) "It is necessary."

Pages 194–196   Pages 207–212   Pages 230–232   Pages 242–244

LEVEL 5

According to Paul, who intercedes for Christians with "groans that words cannot express"?
   a) the angels
   b) Jesus
   c) saints in heaven
   d) the Spirit

LEVEL 6

Who was "a voice of one calling in the desert"?
   a) John the Baptist   c) Ezekiel
   b) Jesus   d) Haggai

LEVEL 7

What Roman official asked Jesus to heal his servant?
   a) a centurion
   b) a general
   c) the proconsul
   d) the governor

Pages 197–199   Pages 213–218   Pages 233–235   Pages 245–247

BIBLE SILVER

What did John the Baptist say he was unworthy of doing for Christ?
- a) bearing His name
- b) untying His sandals
- c) performing His ministry
- d) cooking His supper

LEVEL 9

To which of the following did Jesus not liken the kingdom of heaven?
- a) a fish net
- b) a wedding banquet
- c) a fire
- d) a hidden treasure

LEVEL 10

How much time passed between Jesus' resurrection and His ascension into heaven?
- a) three days
- c) forty days
- b) a week
- d) a year

LEVEL 11

How long did Methuselah, the oldest man, live?
- a) 130 years
- b) 600 years
- c) 969 years
- d) 1,421 years

BIBLE GOLD

Who is known as the "father of all who play the harp"?
- a) David
- b) Jubal
- c) Seth
- d) Asaph

Pages 203–204   Pages 225–228   Pages 239–240   Pages 251–252

THIRTY INTERACTIVE QUIZZES THAT PUT YOU IN THE HOT SEAT

BIBLE TRIVIA

QUIZ 19

What man did God use to lead the Israelites out of the Egyptian Pharaoh's bondage?

a) Adam
b) Jeremiah
c) Moses
d) Lawrence of Arabia

Page 193

Page 206

Page 229

Page 241

LEVEL 2

How did the animals enter Noah's ark?
- a) single file
- b) in pairs
- c) in groups of five
- d) they miraculously materialized inside

LEVEL 3

What was the name of the man from whom Jesus cast many evil spirits?
- a) Army
- c) Squadron
- b) Legion
- d) Troop

BIBLE BRONZE

What physical ailment did Paul have temporarily after his conversion experience?
- a) leprosy
- c) deafness
- b) lameness
- d) blindness

Pages 194–196   Pages 207–212   Pages 230–232   Pages 242–244

LEVEL 5

How quickly will the glorification of the saints, announced by "the last trumpet," take place?
- a) in the twinkling of an eye
- b) as a horse gallops
- c) in a heartbeat
- d) as the eagle swoops

LEVEL 6

The disciples received the Holy Spirit during what special holiday?
- a) the Day of Atonement
- b) Pentecost
- c) Passover
- d) the Feast of Purim

Pages 197–198   Pages 213–216   Pages 233–234   Pages 245–246

LEVEL 7

Where was Saul of Tarsus when he was converted to Christianity?
- a) atop Mars Hill
- b) on the Mediterranean Sea
- c) in Jerusalem
- d) near Damascus

BIBLE SILVER

Complete Jesus' statement about human souls: "The harvest is plentiful..."
- a) "and the time is short."
- b) "but the workers are few."
- c) "for the Lord has blessed."
- d) "with the choicest of fruit."

LEVEL 9

What word did the crowds repeat during Jesus' triumphal entry into Jerusalem?
- a) "Hosanna"
- c) "Holy"
- b) "Hallelujah"
- d) "Honor"

Pages 199–201   Pages 217–222   Pages 235–237   Pages 247–249

LEVEL 10

On what island was the apostle John when he experienced his Revelation?

- a) Crete
- b) Patmos
- c) Sicily
- d) Cyprus

LEVEL 11

What king literally saw "the handwriting on the wall"?

- a) Uzziah
- b) Nebuchadnezzar
- c) Belshazzar
- d) Darius

BIBLE GOLD

Who was the husband of the prophetess Deborah?

- a) Lappidoth
- b) Sisera
- c) Ehud
- d) Jabin

Pages 202–204 Pages 223–228 Pages 238–240 Pages 250–252

THIRTY INTERACTIVE QUIZZES THAT PUT YOU IN THE HOT SEAT

BIBLE TRIVIA

QUIZ 20

LEVEL 1

What Old Testament prophet spent a night in a lions' den?

- a) Jeremiah
- b) Daniel
- c) Joel
- d) Habakkuk

Page 193

Page 206

Page 229

Page 241

LEVEL 2

By interpreting Pharaoh's dreams, Joseph was able to prepare Egypt for what disaster?

- a) famine
- b) flood
- c) earthquake
- d) stock market crash

LEVEL 3

What is the name of the archangel mentioned in Scripture?

- a) Michael
- b) Benjamin
- c) Gabriel
- d) Donatello

BIBLE BRONZE

What Old Testament figure wrestled with God?

- a) Abraham
- b) Isaac
- c) Jacob
- d) Moses

Pages 194–196 Pages 207–212 Pages 230–232 Pages 242–244

LEVEL 5

How did Samuel know that Saul had disobeyed God by failing to completely annihilate the Amalekites?

a) Saul's shifty eyes
b) the sound of livestock
c) Amalekite military stragglers
d) the Urim and Thummim

LEVEL 6

What did a dove bring back to the ark, indicating to Noah that the great floodwaters had receded?

a) a worm
b) a dead fish
c) a head of grain
d) an olive leaf

LEVEL 7

What sound accompanied the Holy Spirit's arrival at Pentecost?

a) a trumpet blast
b) a violent wind
c) a shout of joy
d) an angel choir

Pages 197–199   Pages 213–218   Pages 233–235   Pages 245–247

BIBLE SILVER

According to the apostle Paul, there is no what for "those who are in Christ Jesus"?

- a) condemnation
- b) fear of death
- c) pain and sorrow
- d) sinful desire

LEVEL 9

According to Jesus, what was Satan "from the beginning"?

- a) a deceiver
- c) an enemy
- b) a rebel
- d) a murderer

LEVEL 10

Isaiah prophesied of a time when the nations would beat their swords into what?

- a) plowshares
- c) goblets
- b) anvils
- d) the ground

Pages 200–202   Pages 219–224   Pages 236–238   Pages 248–250

LEVEL 11

When King Xerxes chose Esther as his queen, whom did she replace?

- a) Vashti
- b) Athaliah
- c) Jezebel
- d) Bathsheba

BIBLE GOLD

On what mount did King Saul die?

- a) Nebo
- c) Hermon
- b) Carmel
- d) Gilboa

Pages 203–204 Pages 225–228 Pages 239–240 Pages 251–252

THIRTY INTERACTIVE QUIZZES THAT PUT YOU IN THE HOT SEAT

BIBLE TRIVIA

QUIZ 21

To which of the following animals are Christians compared?

a) hamsters
b) camels
c) sheep
d) elephants

Page 193

Page 206

Page 229

Page 241

LEVEL 2

What was the name of the angel who told Mary she would give birth to Jesus?

- a) Solomon
- c) Gabriel
- b) Rafael
- d) Alexander

LEVEL 3

According to David, God's spiritual cleansing makes us whiter than what?

- a) dried bones
- b) snow
- c) clouds
- d) wool

BIBLE BRONZE

What was Matthew's occupation before he became a disciple of Jesus?

- a) fisherman
- c) physician
- b) merchant
- d) tax collector

Pages 194–196   Pages 207–212   Pages 230–232   Pages 242–244

LEVEL 5

According the apostle Paul, the Christian's body is the what of the Holy Spirit?

a) temple
b) house
c) chariot
d) slave

LEVEL 6

According to Ecclesiastes, when should you "remember your Creator?"

a) "in the days of your youth"
b) "when times of trouble come"
c) "as your years increase"
d) "in joy and in sorrow"

LEVEL 7

What disguise does Satan use to try to fool Christians?

a) a passionate preacher
b) a wounded traveler
c) an angel of light
d) an innocent child

Pages 197–199   Pages 213–218   Pages 233–235   Pages 245–247

BIBLE SILVER

According to the Proverbs, what is "good medicine"?

a) the word of God
b) a good friend
c) a cheerful heart
d) a generous spirit

LEVEL 9

Which prophet was the son of Hannah and Elkanah?

a) Zechariah   c) Elijah
b) Samuel   d) Nathan

LEVEL 10

Where did God instruct Abraham to sacrifice his son Isaac?

a) Sodom   c) the Red Sea
b) Bethel   d) Moriah

Pages 200–202 Pages 219–224 Pages 236–238 Pages 248–250

LEVEL 11

For what offense did Elisha curse some young people of Bethel, resulting in the mauling of forty-two youth by bears?

a) desecrating the Temple
b) using the Lord's name in vain
c) immorality
d) making fun of his baldness

BIBLE GOLD

What current event did Jesus use as an example to emphasize the need for repentance?

a) an earthquake in Jerusalem
b) a tower collapse that killed eighteen people
c) an outbreak of the plague
d) the drowning of seven people in a boat accident

Pages 203–204   Pages 225–228   Pages 239–240   Pages 251–252

BIBLE TRIVIA

THIRTY INTERACTIVE QUIZZES THAT PUT YOU IN THE HOT SEAT

QUIZ 22

LEVEL 1

Why was Jesus' birth to Mary miraculous?

a) She was very old.

b) She was barren.

c) She was a virgin.

d) She already had twenty-two other children.

Page 193   Page 206   Page 229   Page 241

LEVEL 2

What was the punishment for Lot's wife, who looked back on the destruction of Sodom and Gomorrah?

 a) She contracted leprosy.
 b) She was struck blind.
 c) She lost her firstborn son.
 d) She became a pillar of salt.

LEVEL 3

What kind of branches did people spread before Jesus during His "triumphal entry" into Jerusalem?

 a) olive   c) palm
 b) oak   d) sycamore

Pages 194–195   Pages 207–210   Pages 230–231   Pages 242–243

BIBLE BRONZE

Where did Jesus send the evil spirits he cast out of a man called "Legion"?

- a) into the desert
- b) into a herd of pigs
- c) into the tombs
- d) straight into hell

LEVEL 5

What did Jesus say would not prevail against His church?

- a) the sins of mankind
- b) the armies of Satan
- c) the gates of Hades
- d) the forces of evil

LEVEL 6

Whom did Jesus physically drive out of the Temple?

- a) scribes
- b) Pharisees
- c) money changers
- d) Roman soldiers

Pages 196–198   Pages 211–216   Pages 232–234   Pages 244–246

LEVEL 7

According to James, what should a tempted person never say?

    a) "The devil made me do it."
    b) "My own strength shall save me."
    c) "It is of little account."
    d) "God is tempting me."

BIBLE SILVER

Which of the following sounds will not accompany Jesus' Second Coming?

    a) the trumpet of God
    b) mighty hoof beats
    c) the voice of the archangel
    d) a loud command

LEVEL 9

According to the Proverbs, what is worthless "in the day of wrath"?

    a) power   c) fame
    b) wealth   d) idols

Pages 199–201 Pages 217–222 Pages 235–237 Pages 247–249

LEVEL 10

Which of the following was not one of Job's "comforters"?

- a) Eliphaz the Temanite
- b) Bildad the Shuhite
- c) Zophar the Naamathite
- d) Hamor the Hivite

LEVEL 11

Of what was Bartimaeus healed?

- a) leprosy
- b) demon possession
- c) blindness
- d) lameness

BIBLE GOLD

As the book of Acts concludes, where in Rome is the apostle Paul?

- a) Caesar's palace
- b) a dungeon
- c) the Forum
- d) a rented house

Pages 202–204   Pages 223–228   Pages 238–240   Pages 250–252

BIBLE TRIVIA

THIRTY INTERACTIVE QUIZZES THAT PUT YOU IN THE HOT SEAT

QUIZ 23

LEVEL 1

Jesus said, "I am the good" what?
- a) beekeeper
- b) shepherd
- c) fisherman
- d) camel driver

Page 193   Page 206   Page 229   Page 241

LEVEL 2

According to Jesus, who will inherit the earth?
- a) the environmentalists
- b) the merciful
- c) the peacemakers
- d) the meek

LEVEL 3

After the Fall, what did God place around the Tree of Life to keep Adam and Eve away?
- a) hungry lions
- b) a tall fence
- c) cherubim with flaming swords
- d) a deep moat

BIBLE BRONZE

According to the Proverbs, a gentle answer turns away what?
- a) wrath
- b) enemies
- c) arguments
- d) lawsuits

Pages 194–196   Pages 207–212   Pages 230–232   Pages 242–244

LEVEL 5

What name did Jesus give to Simon Peter?
- a) Apollos
- b) Cephas
- c) Demas
- d) Festus

LEVEL 6

Whom did the widow Ruth marry?
- a) Jesse
- c) Elimelech
- b) Boaz
- d) Obed

LEVEL 7

According to Micah, where does God place forgiven sins?
- a) beyond the stars
- b) the pit of hell
- c) the depths of the sea
- d) gloomy dungeons

Pages 197–199 Pages 213–218 Pages 233–235 Pages 245–247

BIBLE SILVER

What were John the Baptist's clothes made of?
- a) fine silk
- b) white linen
- c) woven yarn
- d) camel hair

LEVEL 9

Where did Jonah try to go to avoid God's call to preach?
- a) Nineveh
- c) Joppa
- b) Babylon
- d) Tarshish

LEVEL 10

What convinced the apostle Paul to take the Gospel message to Macedonia?
- a) God's audible voice
- b) a vision of a man requesting help
- c) a letter from Peter
- d) a sign in the sky

Pages 200–202   Pages 219–224   Pages 236–238   Pages 248–250

LEVEL 11

What is Jesus' last statement in the Bible?
a) "Continue in my love."
b) "Remember the Lord your God."
c) "I am coming soon."
d) "My Father's house awaits you."

BIBLE GOLD

Who became king of Judah at age eight, and was commended for turning to God "with all his heart...soul...and strength"?
a) Josiah
b) Amon
c) Manasseh
d) Zedekiah

Pages 203–204   Pages 225–228   Pages 239–240   Pages 251–252

BIBLE TRIVIA

THIRTY INTERACTIVE QUIZZES THAT PUT YOU IN THE HOT SEAT

QUIZ 24

LEVEL 1

What substance did Jesus miraculously walk upon?

a) water
b) clouds
c) fire
d) eggshells

Page 193

Page 206

Page 229

Page 241

LEVEL 2

When did it happen that "God created the heavens and the earth"?

- a) "Billions of years ago..."
- b) "In the fullness of time..."
- c) "In the beginning..."
- d) "From ancient times..."

LEVEL 3

What instrument did David play to soothe King Saul's spirit?

- a) flute
- b) harp
- c) harmonium
- d) tambourine

BIBLE BRONZE

According to the apostle Paul, the Thessalonians were to "greet all the brothers with a holy" what?

- a) hug
- b) kiss
- c) handshake
- d) blessing

Pages 194–196   Pages 207–212   Pages 230–232   Pages 242–244

LEVEL 5

Complete this quotation of Jesus: "Foxes have holes and birds of the air have nests, but the Son of Man…"

  a) "has a beautiful palace in heaven."
  b) "has a small home in Jerusalem."
  c) "has no place to lay His head."
  d) "has twelve disciples to live with."

LEVEL 6

How did Jesus say He was sending out His disciples?

  a) like doves among hawks
  b) like sheep among wolves
  c) like travelers among thieves
  d) like children among bears

Pages 197–198   Pages 213–216   Pages 233–234   Pages 245–246

LEVEL 7

What prophet took an adulterous wife as a symbol of Israel's unfaithfulness?

- a) Daniel
- b) Hosea
- c) Joel
- d) Amos

BIBLE SILVER

In his Revelation, what did John see sitting upon a scarlet beast?

- a) a king
- b) a priest
- c) a prostitute
- d) a demon

LEVEL 9

According to Matthew, what phenomenon accompanied both the death and resurrection of Jesus?

- a) lightning
- b) howling wind
- c) an earthquake
- d) an eclipse

Pages 199–201　Pages 217–222　Pages 235–237　Pages 247–249

LEVEL 10

What did the prophet Elisha request from his mentor, the prophet Elijah?

- a) a double portion of God's Spirit
- b) a scroll of instructions
- c) his sandals
- d) one month together in private

LEVEL 11

Who assisted Joseph of Arimathea in preparing Jesus' body for burial?

- a) Zacchaeus
- c) Cornelius
- b) Bartimaeus
- d) Nicodemus

BIBLE GOLD

What young man fell from a window and died during a long message by Paul?

- a) Eutychus
- c) Erastus
- b) Demetrius
- d) Crispus

Pages 202–204   Pages 223–228   Pages 238–240   Pages 250–252

THIRTY INTERACTIVE QUIZZES THAT PUT YOU IN THE HOT SEAT •

BIBLE TRIVIA

QUIZ 25

LEVEL 1

Jesus said, "I am the" what "of life"?
    a) vitamins
    b) meat
    c) wine
    d) bread

Page 193

Page 206

Page 229

Page 241

LEVEL 2

What city's wall collapsed at the shout of Joshua's army?

- a) Jericho
- b) Babylon
- c) Jerusalem
- d) Beijing

LEVEL 3

What does the shortest verse in the Bible say Jesus did?

- a) smiled
- c) prayed
- b) wept
- d) spoke

BIBLE BRONZE

What kind of seed did Jesus compare to the kingdom of God?

- a) pomegranate
- c) mustard
- b) grape
- d) olive

LEVEL 5

According to the Proverbs, where should lazy people go for wisdom?

- a) the library
- b) the temple
- c) a wheat field
- d) the ant

LEVEL 6

According to the apostle Paul, in trials and hardships Christians are "more than" what?

- a) conquerors
- b) angels
- c) warriors
- d) kings

LEVEL 7

How many righteous people did the city of Sodom need to keep God from destroying it?

- a) one thousand
- b) two hundred
- c) fifty
- d) ten

Pages 197–199   Pages 213–218   Pages 233–235   Pages 245–247

BIBLE SILVER

What man did David have killed in order to take his wife, Bathsheba?

- a) Uriah
- b) Joab
- c) Ziba
- d) Benaiah

LEVEL 9

Whose mother-in-law had a fever healed by Jesus?

- a) Thomas
- b) Simon Peter
- c) Matthew
- d) Judas Iscariot

LEVEL 10

Which minor prophet prophesied that the Messiah would be born in Bethlehem?

- a) Joel
- b) Amos
- c) Micah
- d) Zechariah

Pages 200–202　Pages 219–224　Pages 236–238　Pages 248–250

LEVEL 11

What follower of Jesus met the resurrected Christ on the road to Emmaus?

a) Thomas
b) Nathanael
c) Martha
d) Cleopas

BIBLE GOLD

Why did Pilate's wife advise her husband to leave Jesus alone?

a) She believed Isaiah's prophecies.
b) She had seen Jesus perform miracles.
c) She had had a bad dream.
d) She feared a Galilean revolt.

Pages 203–204   Pages 225–228   Pages 239–240   Pages 251–252

BIBLE TRIVIA

THIRTY INTERACTIVE QUIZZES THAT PUT YOU IN THE HOT SEAT

QUIZ 26

LEVEL 1

What crafty animal convinced Eve to eat the forbidden fruit?

a) cow
b) dove
c) serpent
d) dinosaur

Page 193

Page 206

Page 229

Page 241

LEVEL 2

What kind of water did Jesus offer the Samaritan woman at the well?

a) living

b) cool

c) fresh

d) purified

LEVEL 3

Complete this quotation of Jesus: "Then you will know the truth..."

a) "and the truth will set you free."

b) "and you will be wise."

c) "and many will accept your teaching."

d) "and you will enjoy prosperity."

BIBLE BRONZE

According to the book of Ephesians, it is by what that we are saved?

a) good works

b) grace

c) love

d) tithing

Pages 194–196   Pages 207–212   Pages 230–232   Pages 242–244

LEVEL 5

What was the reaction of ninety-year-old Sarah when the Lord said she would bear a son?

  a) She laughed.   c) She fainted.
  b) She wept.   d) She argued.

LEVEL 6

Which of the following baking items did Jesus compare to the kingdom of heaven?

  a) a pan
  b) flour
  c) an egg
  d) yeast

LEVEL 7

What did Pharaoh and the Egyptians force their Israelite slaves to produce?

  a) armor   c) bricks
  b) wagons   d) idols

Pages 197–199 Pages 213–218 Pages 233–235 Pages 245–247

BIBLE SILVER

On which day of creation did God make birds and fish?

- a) day two
- b) day three
- c) day four
- d) day five

LEVEL 9

Where were the disciples first called "Christians"?

- a) Antioch
- b) Cyprus
- c) Jerusalem
- d) Pamphylia

LEVEL 10

Who initially scoffed at Jesus, saying, "Nazareth! Can anything good come from there?"

- a) Peter
- b) Philip
- c) John
- d) Nathanael

Pages 200–202 Pages 219–224 Pages 236–238 Pages 248–250

LEVEL 11

What sin of David led to a plague that killed seventy thousand Israelites?

- a) his adultery with Bathsheba
- b) the murder of Uriah
- c) counting the Israelites
- d) polygamy

BIBLE GOLD

What famous Bible personality did God name "Jedidiah"?

- a) Noah
- b) Solomon
- c) Jeremiah
- d) Daniel

Pages 203–204 Pages 225–228 Pages 239–240 Pages 251–252

BIBLE TRIVIA

THIRTY INTERACTIVE QUIZZES THAT PUT YOU IN THE HOT SEAT

QUIZ 27

LEVEL 1

Which of the following is not a biblical nationality?

- a) Canaanite
- b) Perizzite
- c) Jebusite
- d) Woolite

Page 193

Page 206

Page 229

Page 241

LEVEL 2

Which of the following was not a gift the wise men brought the baby Jesus?

- a) gold
- b) diamonds
- c) frankincense
- d) myrrh

LEVEL 3

Jesus said, "I am the way, the truth, and the" what?

- a) life
- b) bread
- c) door
- d) Lord

BIBLE BRONZE

How did John the Baptist die?

- a) by crucifixion
- b) by beheading
- c) by stoning
- d) by being torn apart by animals

Pages 194–196   Pages 207–212   Pages 230–232   Pages 242–244

LEVEL 5

otiphar's wife tried to seduce what Old
estament character?

    a) Joshua   c) Jacob

    b) Judah   d) Joseph

LEVEL 6

Who had a vision of heaven as he was being
martyred for his strong preaching?

    a) Stephen   c) Paul

    b) Matthias   d) Timothy

LEVEL 7

According to the book of Romans, how did God
prove his love for sinners?

    a) Noah's rainbow

    b) Christ's death

    c) Paul's conversion

    d) John's Revelation

Pages 197–199   Pages 213–218   Pages 233–235   Pages 245–247

BIBLE SILVER

What prophet rebuked David for his sin with Bathsheba?

- a) Samuel
- b) Iddo
- c) Nathan
- d) Jehu

LEVEL 9

Where did Jesus say Peter would find a coin to pay their temple tax?

- a) along the roadside
- b) in a fish's mouth
- c) in the hem of Peter's robe
- d) on the floor of the Upper Room

LEVEL 10

What man blessed Mary and Joseph as they presented the young Jesus to the Lord?

- a) Phanuel
- b) Simeon
- c) Heli
- d) Jairus

Pages 200–202   Pages 219–224   Pages 236–238   Pages 248–250

LEVEL 11

Who was stoned to death after taking silver and gold from the destroyed city of Jericho?

a) Achan
b) Balak
c) Jephunneh
d) Zelophehad

BIBLE GOLD

What does the name "Barnabas" mean?

a) Devoted to God
b) Son of Encouragement
c) The Lord Saves
d) Man of Faith

Pages 203–204   Pages 225–228   Pages 239–240   Pages 251–252

BIBLE TRIVIA

THIRTY INTERACTIVE QUIZZES THAT PUT YOU IN THE HOT SEAT

QUIZ 28

LEVEL 1

From what substance did God form Adam?

a) chopped figs
b) water
c) dust
d) grass

Page 193   Page 206   Page 229   Page 241

LEVEL 2

On what did God inscribe His Ten Commandments?

- a) a compact disc
- b) papyrus
- c) stone tablets
- d) a leather scroll

LEVEL 3

Jesus said that He is the Alpha and the what?

- a) Beta
- c) Omega
- b) Delta
- d) Sigma

BIBLE BRONZE

For the apostle Paul, "to live is Christ, and to die is" what?

- a) gain
- b) joy
- c) peace
- d) heaven

Pages 194–196   Pages 207–212   Pages 230–232   Pages 242–244

LEVEL 5

How many churches did Jesus address in the book of Revelation?

- a) one
- b) three
- c) seven
- d) twenty-one

LEVEL 6

Which disciples asked to sit at Jesus' right and left hand in heaven?

- a) James and John
- b) Philip and Thomas
- c) Peter and Andrew
- d) Matthew and Simon the Zealot

LEVEL 7

What woman, a seller of purple cloth, was one of the first Christian converts in Philippi?

- a) Lydia
- b) Sapphira
- c) Susanna
- d) Persis

Pages 197–199   Pages 213–218   Pages 233–235   Pages 245–247

BIBLE SILVER

According to the Psalms, what is "the beginning of wisdom"?

    a)   the prayer of faith
    b)   obedience
    c)   the fear of the Lord
    d)   repentance

LEVEL 9

What brothers were known as "Boanerges," or "sons of thunder"?

    a)   Cain and Abel
    b)   Jacob and Esau
    c)   James and John
    d)   Peter and Andrew

Pages 200–201   Pages 219–222   Pages 236–237   Pages 248–249

LEVEL 10

The Jewish celebration of Purim originated with which Bible story?

- a) Esther and Mordecai
- b) David and Goliath
- c) Joshua and the battle of Jericho
- d) Nehemiah and the walls of Jerusalem

LEVEL 11

How many times was the apostle Paul shipwrecked?

- a) none
- b) once
- c) three times
- d) eight times

BIBLE GOLD

Who replaced Judas Iscariot as the twelfth apostle?

- a) John Mark
- b) Justus
- c) Matthias
- d) Luke

Pages 202–204   Pages 223–228   Pages 238–240   Pages 250–252

THIRTY INTERACTIVE QUIZZES THAT PUT YOU IN THE HOT SEAT

BIBLE
TRIVIA

QUIZ 29

LEVEL 1

Which of the following does the Bible say God keeps numbered?

a) the hairs of your head
b) the trees of the forest
c) the fish of the sea
d) the burgers served at McDonalds

Page 193   Page 206   Page 229   Page 241

LEVEL 2

What was the "forbidden fruit" that Adam and Eve ate?

- a) an apple
- b) a fig
- c) a pear
- d) it's not specified

LEVEL 3

What signal did Judas Iscariot use to betray Jesus to His enemies?

- a) a kiss
- b) a hug
- c) a handshake
- d) a nod

BIBLE BRONZE

Who sold his birthright for a meal of bread and lentil stew?

- a) Jacob
- b) Laban
- c) Isaac
- d) Esau

Pages 194–196   Pages 207–212   Pages 230–232   Pages 242–244

LEVEL 5

What man was also known by the name "Israel"?

- a) Adam
- b) Moses
- c) Jacob
- d) David

LEVEL 6

What was Jesus' first miracle?

- a) healing a blind man
- b) raising Lazarus from the dead
- c) walking on water
- d) turning water into wine

LEVEL 7

According to James, faith without what is dead or useless?

- a) love
- b) prayer
- c) God
- d) deeds

Pages 197–199   Pages 213–218   Pages 233–235   Pages 245–247

BIBLE SILVER

What immoral woman is commended in the book of Hebrews for her faith?

- a) Gomer
- b) Rahab
- c) Jezebel
- d) the woman at the well

LEVEL 9

In addition to Jesus, who did the chief priests want to put to death?

- a) Peter
- b) John
- c) Lazarus
- d) Nicodemus

LEVEL 10

When Paul said, "I wish that all men were as I am," he was wishing that they were what?

- a) apostles
- b) missionaries
- c) disciplined
- d) unmarried

Pages 200–202 Pages 219–224 Pages 236–238 Pages 248–250

LEVEL 11

Which of the following is not a food the Israelites craved from Egypt?

- a) cucumbers
- b) melons
- c) onions
- d) apples

BIBLE GOLD

What judge of Israel made a rash vow that led to the sacrifice of his only daughter?

- a) Othniel
- b) Jephthah
- c) Shamgar
- d) Samson

Pages 203–204   Pages 225–228   Pages 239–240   Pages 251–252

BIBLE TRIVIA

THIRTY INTERACTIVE QUIZZES THAT PUT YOU IN THE HOT SEAT

QUIZ 30

LEVEL 1

From what part of Adam did God form Eve?

  a) a thigh bone
  b) a rib
  c) a finger
  d) an ear lobe

Page 193

Page 206

Page 229

Page 241

LEVEL 2

What sacrificial animal shares its name with Jesus?

a) bull

b) dove

c) ram

d) lamb

LEVEL 3

Whose temple offering was commended by Jesus?

a) a wealthy Pharisee's

b) a young child's

c) a beloved priest's

d) a poor widow's

BIBLE BRONZE

Where did Solomon obtain the cedar with which he built the Lord's Temple?

a) Lebanon

b) Sinai

c) Egypt

d) Cyprus

LEVEL 5

What ruler tried to eliminate the baby Jesus by ordering the murder of all boys two years old and younger around Bethlehem?

a) Caesar Augustus   c) Pontius Pilate
b) Tiberius Caesar   d) Herod

LEVEL 6

When the Holy Spirit descended on Jesus after His baptism, how did it appear?

a) like a sparrow
b) like a dove
c) like an eagle
d) like a snowflake

LEVEL 7

What was the name of the boy that Abram fathered by Sarai's maidservant Hagar?

a) Ishmael   c) Issachar
b) Isaac   d) Isaiah

Pages 197–199 Pages 213–218 Pages 233–235 Pages 245–247

BIBLE SILVER

What is the name of the female judge who led Israel to a victory over the Canaanites?

- a) Hannah
- b) Deborah
- c) Abigail
- d) Huldah

LEVEL 9

According to Paul, how many people saw Jesus after His resurrection?

- a) one
- b) twelve
- c) twenty-seven
- d) more than five hundred

LEVEL 10

Where did Jesus move to after leaving Nazareth?

- a) Capernaum
- b) Jerusalem
- c) Cana
- d) Bethany

LEVEL 11

What prophet was thrown into a muddy pit for his discouraging messages?

a) Obadiah
b) Nahum
c) Jeremiah
d) Zephaniah

BIBLE GOLD

What builder's tool did God show Amos to indicate Israel's coming judgment?

a) a chisel
b) a hammer
c) a trowel
d) a plumb line

Pages 203–204   Pages 225–228   Pages 239–240   Pages 251–252

BIBLE
BONUSES

DOUBLE YOUR CHANCES

LEVEL 1

INCORRECT ANSWERS INCLUDE:

Quiz 1—A and D	Quiz 16—B and D
Quiz 2—B and D	Quiz 17—A and B
Quiz 3—C and D	Quiz 18—B and D
Quiz 4—A and B	Quiz 19—A and D
Quiz 5—B and D	Quiz 20—A and C
Quiz 6—C and D	Quiz 21—A and D
Quiz 7—A and D	Quiz 22—B and D
Quiz 8—C and D	Quiz 23—A and D
Quiz 9—A and B	Quiz 24—C and D
Quiz 10—A and D	Quiz 25—A and C
Quiz 11—B and C	Quiz 26—A and D
Quiz 12—A and D	Quiz 27—A and B
Quiz 13—C and D	Quiz 28—A and B
Quiz 14—A and B	Quiz 29—C and D
Quiz 15—A and D	Quiz 30—A and D

DOUBLE YOUR CHANCES

LEVEL 2

INCORRECT ANSWERS INCLUDE:

Quiz 1—A and D

Quiz 2—A and B

Quiz 3—C and D

Quiz 4—A and C

Quiz 5—C and D

Quiz 6—A and D

Quiz 7—A and C

Quiz 8—A and B

Quiz 9—C and D

Quiz 10—A and C

Quiz 11—B and D

Quiz 12—A and D

Quiz 13—A and B

Quiz 14—A and D

Quiz 15—A and C

Quiz 16—B and D

Quiz 17—A and D

Quiz 18—A and B

Quiz 19—C and D

Quiz 20—B and D

Quiz 21—A and D

Quiz 22—B and C

Quiz 23—A and C

Quiz 24—A and D

Quiz 25—C and D

Quiz 26—B and D

Quiz 27—C and D

Quiz 28—A and B

Quiz 29—B and C

Quiz 30—A and C

DOUBLE
YOUR CHANCES

LEVEL 3

INCORRECT ANSWERS INCLUDE:

Quiz 1—B and C

Quiz 2—C and D

Quiz 3—A and D

Quiz 4—B and D

Quiz 5—B and D

Quiz 6—A and B

Quiz 7—A and C

Quiz 8—A and D

Quiz 9—A and C

Quiz 10—A and D

Quiz 11—B and C

Quiz 12—A and C

Quiz 13—B and C

Quiz 14—B and C

Quiz 15—A and C

Quiz 16—A and B

Quiz 17—B and D

Quiz 18—C and D

Quiz 19—A and C

Quiz 20—B and D

Quiz 21—A and D

Quiz 22—A and B

Quiz 23—B and D

Quiz 24—C and D

Quiz 25—A and D

Quiz 26—C and D

Quiz 27—B and C

Quiz 28—B and D

Quiz 29—C and D

Quiz 30—A and B

DOUBLE YOUR CHANCES

BIBLE BRONZE

INCORRECT ANSWERS INCLUDE:

Quiz 1—A and B	Quiz 16—A and B
Quiz 2—A and D	Quiz 17—B and D
Quiz 3—C and D	Quiz 18—B and D
Quiz 4—A and C	Quiz 19—A and C
Quiz 5—B and D	Quiz 20—B and D
Quiz 6—A and D	Quiz 21—B and C
Quiz 7—A and B	Quiz 22—C and D
Quiz 8—C and D	Quiz 23—B and D
Quiz 9—B and C	Quiz 24—A and C
Quiz 10—C and D	Quiz 25—B and D
Quiz 11—B and D	Quiz 26—A and D
Quiz 12—A and C	Quiz 27—C and D
Quiz 13—B and D	Quiz 28—B and C
Quiz 14—B and D	Quiz 29—A and C
Quiz 15—C and D	Quiz 30—C and D

DOUBLE YOUR CHANCES

LEVEL 5

INCORRECT ANSWERS INCLUDE:

Quiz 1—B and D	Quiz 16—A and D
Quiz 2—B and D	Quiz 17—C and D
Quiz 3—A and D	Quiz 18—A and B
Quiz 4—B and C	Quiz 19—B and D
Quiz 5—B and D	Quiz 20—A and C
Quiz 6—A and B	Quiz 21—C and D
Quiz 7—C and D	Quiz 22—A and B
Quiz 8—C and D	Quiz 23—A and D
Quiz 9—B and C	Quiz 24—A and B
Quiz 10—A and B	Quiz 25—A and B
Quiz 11—B and C	Quiz 26—C and D
Quiz 12—B and D	Quiz 27—A and B
Quiz 13—B and C	Quiz 28—A and D
Quiz 14—A and C	Quiz 29—A and B
Quiz 15—A and B	Quiz 30—B and C

DOUBLE YOUR CHANCES

LEVEL 6

INCORRECT ANSWERS INCLUDE:

Quiz 1—C and D

Quiz 2—B and D

Quiz 3—A and C

Quiz 4—B and C

Quiz 5—A and C

Quiz 6—A and B

Quiz 7—B and D

Quiz 8—A and D

Quiz 9—A and B

Quiz 10—C and D

Quiz 11—A and B

Quiz 12—A and D

Quiz 13—B and D

Quiz 14—B and C

Quiz 15—A and C

Quiz 16—A and B

Quiz 17—A and B

Quiz 18—C and D

Quiz 19—A and C

Quiz 20—A and B

Quiz 21—B and C

Quiz 22—A and D

Quiz 23—C and D

Quiz 24—A and C

Quiz 25—C and D

Quiz 26—A and B

Quiz 27—C and D

Quiz 28—B and D

Quiz 29—B and C

Quiz 30—C and D

DOUBLE YOUR CHANCES

LEVEL 7

INCORRECT ANSWERS INCLUDE:

Quiz 1—A and D

Quiz 2—A and B

Quiz 3—C and D

Quiz 4—A and C

Quiz 5—A and D

Quiz 6—A and B

Quiz 7—C and D

Quiz 8—A and C

Quiz 9—C and D

Quiz 10—B and C

Quiz 11—A and B

Quiz 12—B and C

Quiz 13—B and D

Quiz 14—A and B

Quiz 15—A and D

Quiz 16—C and D

Quiz 17—B and C

Quiz 18—B and D

Quiz 19—A and B

Quiz 20—C and D

Quiz 21—B and D

Quiz 22—A and C

Quiz 23—A and D

Quiz 24—A and C

Quiz 25—B and C

Quiz 26—B and D

Quiz 27—C and D

Quiz 28—B and D

Quiz 29—B and C

Quiz 30—B and D

DOUBLE YOUR CHANCES

BIBLE SILVER

INCORRECT ANSWERS INCLUDE:

Quiz 1—C and D	Quiz 16—B and C
Quiz 2—A and C	Quiz 17—B and D
Quiz 3—A and B	Quiz 18—C and D
Quiz 4—B and C	Quiz 19—A and D
Quiz 5—B and C	Quiz 20—C and D
Quiz 6—C and D	Quiz 21—B and D
Quiz 7—A and B	Quiz 22—A and C
Quiz 8—A and D	Quiz 23—A and B
Quiz 9—C and D	Quiz 24—B and D
Quiz 10—B and D	Quiz 25—B and C
Quiz 11—A and C	Quiz 26—A and C
Quiz 12—B and C	Quiz 27—A and D
Quiz 13—B and D	Quiz 28—B and D
Quiz 14—A and B	Quiz 29—A and C
Quiz 15—A and C	Quiz 30—A and C

DOUBLE YOUR CHANCES

LEVEL 9

INCORRECT ANSWERS INCLUDE:

Quiz 1—A and D	Quiz 16—C and D
Quiz 2—C and D	Quiz 17—B and D
Quiz 3—B and D	Quiz 18—B and D
Quiz 4—A and B	Quiz 19—B and C
Quiz 5—A and C	Quiz 20—A and B
Quiz 6—B and D	Quiz 21—A and D
Quiz 7—C and D	Quiz 22—C and D
Quiz 8—A and B	Quiz 23—A and B
Quiz 9—B and C	Quiz 24—B and D
Quiz 10—B and D	Quiz 25—A and C
Quiz 11—A and D	Quiz 26—B and D
Quiz 12—B and C	Quiz 27—A and D
Quiz 13—A and D	Quiz 28—A and B
Quiz 14—C and D	Quiz 29—B and D
Quiz 15—A and B	Quiz 30—A and C

DOUBLE
YOUR CHANCES

LEVEL 10

INCORRECT ANSWERS INCLUDE:

Quiz 1—C and D

Quiz 2—A and C

Quiz 3—A and D

Quiz 4—A and C

Quiz 5—B and D

Quiz 6—A and B

Quiz 7—C and D

Quiz 8—B and C

Quiz 9—B and D

Quiz 10—A and D

Quiz 11—B and D

Quiz 12—A and B

Quiz 13—A and C

Quiz 14—B and C

Quiz 15—A and D

Quiz 16—B and D

Quiz 17—A and B

Quiz 18—B and D

Quiz 19—C and D

Quiz 20—C and D

Quiz 21—A and B

Quiz 22—B and C

Quiz 23—C and D

Quiz 24—C and D

Quiz 25—A and B

Quiz 26—B and C

Quiz 27—C and D

Quiz 28—B and D

Quiz 29—A and C

Quiz 30—C and D

DOUBLE YOUR CHANCES

LEVEL 11

INCORRECT ANSWERS INCLUDE:

Quiz 1—B and C

Quiz 2—C and D

Quiz 3—A and D

Quiz 4—B and D

Quiz 5—A and B

Quiz 6—B and C

Quiz 7—A and C

Quiz 8—C and D

Quiz 9—A and D

Quiz 10—B and C

Quiz 11—A and D

Quiz 12—B and D

Quiz 13—C and D

Quiz 14—A and B

Quiz 15—A and C

Quiz 16—B and D

Quiz 17—C and D

Quiz 18—B and D

Quiz 19—A and D

Quiz 20—C and D

Quiz 21—B and C

Quiz 22—A and D

Quiz 23—B and D

Quiz 24—B and C

Quiz 25—A and B

Quiz 26—B and D

Quiz 27—C and D

Quiz 28—A and D

Quiz 29—B and C

Quiz 30—A and B

DOUBLE
YOUR CHANCES

BIBLE GOLD

INCORRECT ANSWERS INCLUDE:

Quiz 1—A and D
Quiz 2—A and C
Quiz 3—B and C
Quiz 4—C and D
Quiz 5—A and B
Quiz 6—B and D
Quiz 7—C and D
Quiz 8—A and D
Quiz 9—B and D
Quiz 10—B and C
Quiz 11—C and D
Quiz 12—B and C
Quiz 13—A and B
Quiz 14—A and C
Quiz 15—A and D

Quiz 16—C and D
Quiz 17—B and D
Quiz 18—C and D
Quiz 19—B and C
Quiz 20—A and C
Quiz 21—C and D
Quiz 22—B and C
Quiz 23—C and D
Quiz 24—B and C
Quiz 25—A and D
Quiz 26—A and D
Quiz 27—A and C
Quiz 28—B and D
Quiz 29—A and D
Quiz 30—A and C

HAVE A HINT

LEVEL 1

Quiz 1—He's first alphabetically, too.

Quiz 2—You know a clue's in this sentence...

Quiz 3—King _____, Star of _____.

Quiz 4—Though she had the name, she was not "quite contrary."

Quiz 5—Good luck finding these posted on a school wall.

Quiz 6—Maybe he met her late in the day.

Quiz 7—Phone a buddy for help on this one...

Quiz 8—This is not a trick question—it's really that easy!

Quiz 9—If he's been portrayed by Charlton Heston, he's the one.

Quiz 10—And God said, "Don't sweat it."

Quiz 11—Don't you love a Sunday afternoon nap?

Quiz 12—With Jesus, they made a baker's dozen.

Quiz 13—He zigged, and zagged, and zipped through the crowd.

Quiz 14—A sensitive, sympathetic servant.

Quiz 15—He was "cool," not "sloppy."

Quiz 16—Starts like a common name of a girl.

Quiz 17—A certain celestial signal...

Quiz 18—Where there was no danger from a stranger...

Quiz 19—The Israelites mosied on down behind him.

Quiz 20—Think: Boone, Defoe, or Webster.

Quiz 21—Is that before or after we've been shorn?

Quiz 22—Some popular Caribbean islands share a word in this answer.

Quiz 23—It would be baaaaaaad if you missed this one.

Quiz 24—You can walk on it, too—if it's frozen.

Quiz 25—White or wheat?

Quiz 26—Surely a slithering, sneaky sort.

Quiz 27—Yes, you clean your sweaters with this.

Quiz 28—You might have swept the raw materials under your rug.

Quiz 29—Michael Jordan and Captain Picard make it easy for God...

Quiz 30—It was not barbecued.

HAVE A HINT

LEVEL 2

Quiz 1—He later was his own judge and jury.

Quiz 2—It might begin, "Because..."

Quiz 3—You might find his name on your luggage.

Quiz 4—God is there when life gets woolly.

Quiz 5—In heaven, our most valuable stuff is pavement.

Quiz 6—Wood you like to take a guess?

Quiz 7—These critters aren't sacred.

Quiz 8—He shares a name with one of the Brady kids.

Quiz 9—John Steinbeck wrote of being "East of" there.

Quiz 10—No one gets left out...

Quiz 11—The "pot of gold" tradition came much later.

Quiz 12—So long and good-bye.

Quiz 13—It's "blue" in a classical waltz.

Quiz 14—Consider this: It fires a stone.

Quiz 15—They couldn't hold up their execution.

Quiz 16—At first, she seemed delightful.

Quiz 17—Add "Lee" for a dessert maker.

Quiz 18—Direct from God's kitchen...

Quiz 19—Mr. and Mrs., side by side.

Quiz 20—Hear that rumble? It's the sound of stomachs growling.

Quiz 21—As a talker, maybe he had the "gift of ___."

Quiz 22—Put that in a shaker!

Quiz 23—Like mild-mannered reporter Clark Kent...

Quiz 24—Why not start at the start?

Quiz 25—How's your knowledge of spirituals? "Joshua fit the battle of...."

Quiz 26—Animate, vital.

Quiz 27—They might be a girl's best friend, but the wise men weren't impressed.

Quiz 28—Built to last...

Quiz 29—Left to the imagination...

Quiz 30—Think: sweet and innocent.

HAVE A HINT

LEVEL 3

Quiz 1—It was death, not laziness.

Quiz 2—That river had a lot of momentum.

Quiz 3—Think: chore.

Quiz 4—Like going from Don to Ron.

Quiz 5—Twelve-inch measurements...

Quiz 6—Pssst...I've got a secret!

Quiz 7—Arborvitae? Rhododendron? Rose?

Quiz 8—Think: Baseball's "Hammerin' Hank."

Quiz 9—There's a type of apple with this name.

Quiz 10—Rivers and financial institutions have them.

Quiz 11—You'll typically notice it early in the morning.

Quiz 12—Think: hotel room Bibles.

Quiz 13—He has a farm building in his name.

Quiz 14—Easy, now...

Quiz 15—Joyful enthusiasm accompanied their birth.

Quiz 16—May I have a _____ with you?

Quiz 17—It's not a request.

Quiz 18—We all have them on our legs.

Quiz 19—There are "American" and "French Foreign" versions.

Quiz 20—Add "angelo," and you've got a classical painter.

Quiz 21—It can go with "plow" or "ball."

Quiz 22—Some grow coconuts.

Quiz 23—Guardian angels...

Quiz 24—Add "oon" for a whaling spear.

Quiz 25—His friend had just died.

Quiz 26—American slaves liked to quote this verse.

Quiz 27—Your very heartbeat...

Quiz 28—An Irish million?

Quiz 29—The intimacy made the betrayal especially painful.

Quiz 30—It wasn't the size of the offering—it was the percentage.

HAVE A HINT

BIBLE BRONZE

Quiz 1—That sin is very serious stuff.

Quiz 2—Despite the sound of his name, he never flew an airplane.

Quiz 3—He also wrote the fourth Gospel.

Quiz 4—Troublemakers "raise" him.

Quiz 5—They're sweet, tender, and good for you.

Quiz 6—Remember, we're dealing with character qualities.

Quiz 7—Think: Barbie's boyfriend.

Quiz 8—Since there's no more death, it's...

Quiz 9—It sounds like confused chatter.

Quiz 10—He shares a name with a cactus the size of a tree.

Quiz 11—On an altar...

Quiz 12—A new kind of angler.

Quiz 13—Remember that God is a jealous God.

Quiz 14—Some say bad things come in threes.

Quiz 15—Like the Tour de France.

Quiz 16—It was a pretty smart request.

Quiz 17—Hymn title: "_____ Is the Victory."

Quiz 18—Mission accomplished.

Quiz 19—Like Fanny Crosby or Stevie Wonder.

Quiz 20—God would take him down, shake him up, make him new.

Quiz 21—He was not a popular guy.

Quiz 22—Those aren't squeals of delight...

Quiz 23—Add an "e" for a Christmas decoration.

Quiz 24—But not from Hershey's.

Quiz 25—French's or Grey Poupon might be interested.

Quiz 26—You might "say" it before dinner.

Quiz 27—Like Louis XVI and Marie Antoinette.

Quiz 28—As opposed to loss...

Quiz 29—He saw no value in the birthright.

Quiz 30—Where you'll find Beirut today.

HAVE A HINT

LEVEL 5

Quiz 1—Ironically, he first saw her bathing.

Quiz 2—It'll sneak up on you.

Quiz 3—Talk about a tight fit!

Quiz 4—"Doubting" is part of his name.

Quiz 5—He was at the end of his rope...

Quiz 6—Sounds like a chest-beating jungle hero...

Quiz 7—Think: "Jesus of _____."

Quiz 8—A special place...

Quiz 9—Shout "_____, hallelujah!"

Quiz 10—Belief in the unseen.

Quiz 11—Shares a name with a peninsula.

Quiz 12—Key word in question: "Visiting."

Quiz 13—An unusual paint job...

Quiz 14—The Beatles said it's all you need.

Quiz 15—Zoos have them, too.

Quiz 16—Think: TV sitcom island...

Quiz 17—It cuts both ways.

Quiz 18—The third person of the Trinity.

Quiz 19—A mark of a merry person.

Quiz 20—Lowing and bleating.

Quiz 21—Like a church...

Quiz 22—Beating the doors down...
Quiz 23—Jesus called him a "rock"—like cement?
Quiz 24—Think: nomadic.
Quiz 25—Hold a picnic and he'll come to you...
Quiz 26—Like she'd just heard a punch line...
Quiz 27—Think: DiMaggio or Stalin.
Quiz 28—The square root of 49.
Quiz 29—His name goes with "ladder."
Quiz 30—He was horrid...

HAVE A HINT

LEVEL 6

Quiz 1—Grief, anguish, woe.

Quiz 2—Think: Asimov or Bashevis Singer.

Quiz 3—Cupidity, avarice, greed.

Quiz 4—With a smile!

Quiz 5—Shazaam—a talking donkey?

Quiz 6—The first shall be last.

Quiz 7—Like riding a spiritual elevator…

Quiz 8—Slightly over 16 percent.

Quiz 9—You should do this before dinner, too.

Quiz 10—Jesus is always the best example.

Quiz 11—Not all advice is good advice.

Quiz 12—Comprehension.

Quiz 13—His eye is on it.

Quiz 14—One-ninth of a year!

Quiz 15—We're talking lots (and lots) of wives.

Quiz 16—Probably the least impressive way…

Quiz 17—Filet mignon, anyone?

Quiz 18—He shares a name with another key Bible character.

Quiz 19—Think: Five-sided things.

Quiz 20—A symbol of peace.

Quiz 21—Before you're long in the tooth...
Quiz 22—Yen to pounds to francs, etc.
Quiz 23—Think: constrictorz.
Quiz 24—Bo Peep's among Big Bads.
Quiz 25—Like William the...
Quiz 26—Also known as leaven.
Quiz 27—Think: Lincoln's opponent Douglas.
Quiz 28—Carter and Kennedy...
Quiz 29—A sort of alchemy?
Quiz 30—A symbol of peace.

HAVE A HINT

LEVEL 7

Quiz 1—A man's home is his embassy.

Quiz 2—Mind your manners: Say _____.

Quiz 3—Sounds like a PLO leader.

Quiz 4—Think: Big diamond at the Smithsonian...

Quiz 5—It's the only one who shares a name with a biblical book.

Quiz 6—The King James might say, "A man diest."

Quiz 7—Like Androcles's lion friend.

Quiz 8—Knock, knock. Who's there?

Quiz 9—Atheists, et al.

Quiz 10—Judas had tried to return the money, in vein.

Quiz 11—Is it getting hot in here?

Quiz 12—United in spirit...and body.

Quiz 13—It was his major claim to fame.

Quiz 14—He was the disciples' treasurer...

Quiz 15—Quite an irony, actually.

Quiz 16—And perhaps his tight stomach muscles...

Quiz 17—Heads up!

Quiz 18—Think: "penny."

Quiz 19—In present-day Syria.

Quiz 20—An F-4 or F-5, perhaps?

Quiz 21—He's pretty bright…

Quiz 22—Don't blame the blameless.

Quiz 23—Where not even the *Red October* could find them.

Quiz 24—"_____ can you see, by the dawn's early light?"

Quiz 25—One for each dime in a dollar.

Quiz 26—For those pyramids, perhaps?

Quiz 27—This love covered a multitude of sins.

Quiz 28—Think: Moammar Kadaffi's country…

Quiz 29—Just do it.

Quiz 30—He shares a name with *Moby Dick*'s narrator.

HAVE A HINT

BIBLE SILVER

Quiz 1—And never the two shall meet...

Quiz 2—He's a king, all right.

Quiz 3—Jesus saw right through the temptation...

Quiz 4—Think: indent key.

Quiz 5—It's more than an emotion.

Quiz 6—But nobody wrote a biblical book to them.

Quiz 7—First person, present tense.

Quiz 8—Think: ice cream and root beer...

Quiz 9—Think: Diller or Schlafly.

Quiz 10—I can't get no satisfaction...

Quiz 11—Say what?

Quiz 12—Let's ask Bill Gates.

Quiz 13—Think: President Jackson.

Quiz 14—As pie, so they say.

Quiz 15—The final and most serious...

Quiz 16—Legionnaires.

Quiz 17—"I am the light of the world."

Quiz 18—Today, he'd use Velcro.

Quiz 19—Economists call it a labor shortage.

Quiz 20—Censure or blame.

Quiz 21—Modern proverbs say laughter is the best medicine.

220

Quiz 22—No chariots of fire this time.
Quiz 23—John was a rough, outdoorsy type.
Quiz 24—Strumpet, harlot.
Quiz 25—Shares a name with the Dickens' character Heep.
Quiz 26—Shortly before humans, who were last.
Quiz 27—Shares a name with U.S. patriot Hale.
Quiz 28—But not the kind that makes you scream.
Quiz 29—Sounds like a place for recovering alcoholics...
Quiz 30—Think: Pat Boone's daughter.

HAVE A HINT

LEVEL 9

Level 9

Quiz 1—Philadelphia is the City of…

Quiz 2—Perhaps named after an Old Testament forefather?

Quiz 3—A real word picture.

Quiz 4—America's favorite uncle…

Quiz 5—If you can pronounce it, move to the head of the class.

Quiz 6—Like Heber's famous hymn.

Quiz 7—Abel's death…

Quiz 8—At nine in the morning?

Quiz 9—He made a mockery of the gift of grace.

Quiz 10—It follows the Song of Solomon.

Quiz 11—Gobletman.

Quiz 12—Add an "e" for a man's name.

Quiz 13—But they didn't wear jeans when they worked.

Quiz 14—With his closest associates…

Quiz 15—One of Ben Franklin's two certainties…

Quiz 16—Sometimes it's forked.

Quiz 17—There's a Jane Austen title in the name.

Quiz 18—Chicago had a big one in 1871.

Quiz 19—Think:"_____ Karenina."

Quiz 20—Cain followed in his footsteps.

Quiz 21—A cartoon character from Yosemite shares his name.

Quiz 22—It can't buy you love, either.

Quiz 23—Big fish for _____.

Quiz 24—It predated the Richter Scale.

Quiz 25—He took a brief walk on the wet side.

Quiz 26—It's not really "against" anything...

Quiz 27—Where you'd sometimes find a hook.

Quiz 28—The sons of Zebedee.

Quiz 29—They wanted to keep a good man down...

Quiz 30—More than the miles of Indianapolis...

HAVE A HINT

LEVEL 10

Quiz 1—Think: The study of God.

Quiz 2—No spelunking required.

Quiz 3—A biblical author...

Quiz 4—He shared a name with Peter.

Quiz 5—There's a fishing pole in his name.

Quiz 6—Add an "ng" to determine who did him in.

Quiz 7—Like a firm parent with a picky child...

Quiz 8—A real difficulty for Copernicus.

Quiz 9—Pup or circus?

Quiz 10—He's generally known as the most aggressive, anyway.

Quiz 11—A city that would later host the first modern Olympics.

Quiz 12—Mobile meals?

Quiz 13—Think: A modern musical genre.

Quiz 14—Perhaps from the Napa Valley?

Quiz 15—No man can serve two masters...

Quiz 16—Sounds like the famous quarterback "Broadway Joe."

Quiz 17—Figuratively, it's good luck for an actor.

Quiz 18—A day for each year of the Israelite's wilderness wanderings.

Quiz 19—Think: 700 Club's Robertson.

Quiz 20—Agricultural instruments.

Quiz 21—What more could God ask?

Quiz 22—Avoid alliterating appellations...

Quiz 23—Like someone dialing 911.

Quiz 24—Gimme another...

Quiz 25—Did people want to "be like" him?

Quiz 26—Shares a name with the novelist Hawthorne.

Quiz 27—Shares a name with a tribe of Israel.

Quiz 28—It's a relative thing...

Quiz 29—Think: Bachelor.

Quiz 30—Think: Baseball headwear.

HAVE A HINT

LEVEL 11

Quiz 1—Sounds like partway to somewhere.

Quiz 2—He has a machine gun in his name.

Quiz 3—No work for the sandman.

Quiz 4—Add an "H" for an old-fashioned cheer.

Quiz 5—Think: Street.

Quiz 6—He was too busy fighting off trials.

Quiz 7—She was pregnant for at least sixty-three months (total!).

Quiz 8—Sounds like a bumblebee…

Quiz 9—That's called "immunity"!

Quiz 10—He could have gotten death.

Quiz 11—He interpreted the "handwriting on the wall."

Quiz 12—It was his only claim to fame.

Quiz 13—Sounds like a bad grade in school…

Quiz 14—Normally, that would hurt!

Quiz 15—The same guy who had anointed him king…

Quiz 16—Jesus said to him, "Feed my sheep."

Quiz 17—Supposedly, they "are forever."

Quiz 18—He just missed the millenary.

Quiz 19—This name has a "ring" to it.

Quiz 20—The first queen had acted rashly.

Quiz 21—If you can't say something nice, don't say anything at all.

Quiz 22—His rods and cones weren't working.

Quiz 23—A promise—and a warning?

Quiz 24—He had had a personal sermon on being "born again."

Quiz 25—It's all we know about this person.

Quiz 26—Take a number...

Quiz 27—He was feeling like his name...

Quiz 28—They say it's a crowd...

Quiz 29—How would they keep the doctors away?

Quiz 30—A 60s song said he was a bullfrog...

HAVE
A HINT

BIBLE GOLD

Quiz 1—Today he's a well-known cookie maker.

Quiz 2—Jesus said it was neither hot nor cold—though there's something freezing in its name.

Quiz 3—Sounds like: _____-Seltzer.

Quiz 4—...by the Fourth of July–ah.

Quiz 5— They just don't have a ring to them.

Quiz 6—He sounds like a third-place kind of guy (primary, secondary...).

Quiz 7—No STP needed.

Quiz 8—I'd be really pleased if you could guess this!

Quiz 9—Puff, the Magic...?

Quiz 10—You're toast!

Quiz 11—That's a pretty fair family.

Quiz 12—Just outside the promised land.

Quiz 13—Its days were "numbered."

Quiz 14—This name came in twos, too.

Quiz 15—MGM would be disappointed.

Quiz 16—When their mother called them "big boys," she meant it.

Quiz 17—Did you muster an answer?

Quiz 18—Think: white sphere on a pool table.

Quiz 19—What do you have when sitting that you don't have when standing?

Quiz 20—Were there snakes there?

Quiz 21—Think: Sears, Trump, CN.

Quiz 22—Paul's "bachelor pad."

Quiz 23—Eight years old? No joke.

Quiz 24—What if that happened to you?

Quiz 25—What would Freud have thought?

Quiz 26—If you get this, you're pretty smart!

Quiz 27—People loved to be around him.

Quiz 28—He might have occasionally gotten the tax collector's mail...

Quiz 29—Think: Confederate president.

Quiz 30—To show the straight and true...

LOOK IN THE BOOK

LEVEL 1

Quiz 1—Genesis 2:20

Quiz 2—Genesis 7:1–2

Quiz 3—1 Samuel 17:4, 50

Quiz 4—Matthew 1:16

Quiz 5—Exodus 20:1–21

Quiz 6—Genesis 3:20

Quiz 7—Jonah 1:17

Quiz 8—Genesis 17:5

Quiz 9—Luke 6:13–16

Quiz 10—Daniel 3

Quiz 11—Genesis 2:2

Quiz 12—Luke 6:13

Quiz 13—Luke 19:2–4

Quiz 14—Luke 10:29–37

Quiz 15—Genesis 37:3

Quiz 16—Luke 2:4–6

Quiz 17—Matthew 2:9

Quiz 18—Luke 2:16

Quiz 19—Exodus 6:13

Quiz 20—Daniel 6

Quiz 21—John 10:14

Quiz 22—Matthew 1:23

Quiz 23—John 10:14

Quiz 24—John 6:19

Quiz 25—John 6:35

Quiz 26—Genesis 3:1–6

Quiz 27—Joshua 24:11

Quiz 28—Genesis 2:7

Quiz 29—Matthew 10:30

Quiz 30—Genesis 2:21

LOOK IN
THE BOOK

LEVEL 2

Quiz 1—Matthew 26:14–15
Quiz 2—John 3:16
Quiz 3—Judges 16:6, 17
Quiz 4—Psalm 23:1
Quiz 5—Revelation 21:21
Quiz 6—Matthew 13:55
Quiz 7—Psalm 50:10
Quiz 8—Matthew 26:75
Quiz 9—Genesis 2:8
Quiz 10—Romans 3:23
Quiz 11—Genesis 9:16
Quiz 12—Genesis 19:24
Quiz 13—Genesis 2:10–14
Quiz 14—1 Samuel
   17:48–49
Quiz 15—Matthew 27:38

Quiz 16—Judges 16:18
Quiz 17—Genesis 17:15
Quiz 18—Exodus 16:31
Quiz 19—Genesis 7:8–9
Quiz 20—Genesis 41:25–28
Quiz 21—Luke 1:26–27
Quiz 22—Genesis 19:26
Quiz 23—Matthew 5:5
Quiz 24—Genesis 1:1
Quiz 25—Joshua 6:1, 20
Quiz 26—John 4:10
Quiz 27—Matthew 2:11
Quiz 28—Exodus 31:18
Quiz 29—Genesis 3:6
Quiz 30—John 1:29

LOOK IN THE BOOK

LEVEL 3

LOOK IN THE BOOK

BIBLE BRONZE

Quiz 1—Romans 6:23

Quiz 2—John 19:16

Quiz 3—Revelation 1:9–11

Quiz 4—Genesis 4:8

Quiz 5—Galatians 5:22–23

Quiz 6—Galatians 5:22–23

Quiz 7—Genesis 9:18

Quiz 8—Revelation 21:27

Quiz 9—Genesis 11:9

Quiz 10—Numbers 27:22–23

Quiz 11—Genesis 22:2

Quiz 12—Matthew 4:19

Quiz 13—Exodus 20:3

Quiz 14—Revelation 13:18

Quiz 15—2 Timothy 4:7

Quiz 16—2 Chronicles 1:10

Quiz 17—Romans 1:17

Quiz 18—John 19:30

Quiz 19—Acts 9:9

Quiz 20—Genesis 32:24–28

Quiz 21—Matthew 9:9

Quiz 22—Mark 5:12–13

Quiz 23—Proverbs 15:1

Quiz 24—1 Thessalonians 5:26

Quiz 25—Luke 13:18–19

Quiz 26—Ephesians 2:8

Quiz 27—Matthew 14:10

Quiz 28—Philippians 1:21

Quiz 29—Genesis 25:34

Quiz 30—1 Kings 5:8–9

LOOK IN THE BOOK

LEVEL 5

LOOK IN THE BOOK

LEVEL 6

LOOK IN THE BOOK

LEVEL 7

LOOK IN THE BOOK

BIBLE SILVER

Quiz 1—Psalm 103:12

Quiz 2—Isaiah 38:5

Quiz 3—Matthew 4:1–10

Quiz 4—Acts 9:40

Quiz 5—1 Corinthians 13:8

Quiz 6—Acts 17:10–11

Quiz 7—Exodus 3:14

Quiz 8—2 Kings 6:6

Quiz 9—1 Samuel 17:4

Quiz 10—1 Timothy 6:6

Quiz 11—James 3:8

Quiz 12—Proverbs 22:1

Quiz 13—Mark 14:32–33

Quiz 14—Matthew 11:30

Quiz 15—Revelation 6:1–8

Quiz 16—John 19:2

Quiz 17—John 8:12

Quiz 18—Luke 3:16

Quiz 19—Matthew 9:37

Quiz 20—Romans 8:1

Quiz 21—Proverbs 17:22

Quiz 22—1 Thessalonians 4:16

Quiz 23—Matthew 3:4

Quiz 24—Revelation 17:1–3

Quiz 25—2 Samuel 11:3, 15

Quiz 26—Genesis 1:20–23

Quiz 27—2 Samuel 12:7

Quiz 28—Psalm 111:10

Quiz 29—Hebrews 11:31

Quiz 30—Judges 4:4, 24

LOOK IN THE BOOK

LEVEL 9

Quiz 1—John 13:35
Quiz 2—Mark 15:43
Quiz 3—Matthew 27:33
Quiz 4—Luke 9:30–31
Quiz 5—Hebrews 5:6
Quiz 6—Isaiah 6:3
Quiz 7—Genesis 4:25
Quiz 8—Acts 2:13
Quiz 9—Acts 8:20
Quiz 10—Acts 8:30
Quiz 11—Nehemiah 1:11
Quiz 12—1 Samuel 18:27
Quiz 13—Numbers 1:50–51
Quiz 14—Mark 6:4
Quiz 15—Luke 20:21–25
Quiz 16—Proverbs 18:21
Quiz 17—Luke 24:13–16

Quiz 18—Matthew 13:44, 47; 22:2
Quiz 19—Matthew 21:9
Quiz 20—John 8:44
Quiz 21—1 Samuel 1:19–20
Quiz 22—Proverbs 11:4
Quiz 23—Jonah 1:3
Quiz 24—Matthew 27:51, 28:2
Quiz 25—Mark 1:30–31
Quiz 26—Acts 11:26
Quiz 27—Matthew 17:27
Quiz 28—Mark 3:17
Quiz 29—John 12:10
Quiz 30—1 Corinthians 15:6

LOOK IN THE BOOK

LEVEL 10

Quiz 1—Acts 1:1
Quiz 2—Daniel 4:33
Quiz 3—Acts 15:37–38
Quiz 4—Mark 15:21
Quiz 5—Genesis 10:9
Quiz 6—Esther 7:10
Quiz 7—2 Thessalonians 3:10
Quiz 8—Joshua 10:13
Quiz 9—Acts 18:3
Quiz 10—John 20:4–6
Quiz 11—Acts 17: 22–23
Quiz 12—Acts 10:9–28
Quiz 13—Daniel 2:32–34
Quiz 14—1 Timothy 5:23
Quiz 15—James 4:4

Quiz 16—2 Kings 5:11
Quiz 17—John 19:32
Quiz 18—Acts 1:3
Quiz 19—Revelation 1:9
Quiz 20—Isaiah 2:4
Quiz 21—Genesis 22:2
Quiz 22—Job 2:11
Quiz 23—Acts 16:9–10
Quiz 24—2 Kings 2:9
Quiz 25—Micah 5:2
Quiz 26—John 1:46
Quiz 27—Luke 2:21–35
Quiz 28—Esther 9:31
Quiz 29—1 Corinthians 7:7–8
Quiz 30—Matthew 4:13

LOOK IN THE BOOK

LEVEL 11

Quiz 1—Exodus 2:15
Quiz 2—Isaiah 6:1–8
Quiz 3—Ecclesiastes 3:1–8
Quiz 4—2 Samuel 6:6–7
Quiz 5—Acts 12:13
Quiz 6—Proverbs 1:1, 30:1, 31:1
Quiz 7—Mark 6:3
Quiz 8—Job 1:1
Quiz 9—Acts 28:1–6
Quiz 10—2 Samuel 9:13
Quiz 11—Daniel 1:7
Quiz 12—Acts 23:12–16
Quiz 13—Acts 19:23–34
Quiz 14—Isaiah 6:6–7
Quiz 15—1 Samuel 28:11
Quiz 16—Acts 5:15

Quiz 17—Revelation 21:19–20
Quiz 18—Genesis 5:27
Quiz 19—Daniel 5
Quiz 20—Esther 2:17
Quiz 21—2 Kings 2:23–24
Quiz 22—Mark 10:46, 52
Quiz 23—Revelation 22:20
Quiz 24—John 19:39
Quiz 25—Luke 24:18
Quiz 26—1 Chronicles 21:1, 14
Quiz 27—Joshua 7:20–25
Quiz 28—2 Corinthians 11:25
Quiz 29—Numbers 11:5
Quiz 30—Jeremiah 38:4–6

LOOK IN THE BOOK

BIBLE GOLD

ANSWERS

LEVEL 1

Quiz 1—B

Quiz 2—C

Quiz 3—A

Quiz 4—D

Quiz 5—C

Quiz 6—A

Quiz 7—C

Quiz 8—A

Quiz 9—C

Quiz 10—B

Quiz 11—D

Quiz 12—B

Quiz 13—A

Quiz 14—C

Quiz 15—B

Quiz 16—A

Quiz 17—D

Quiz 18—C

Quiz 19—C

Quiz 20—B

Quiz 21—C

Quiz 22—C

Quiz 23—B

Quiz 24—A

Quiz 25—D

Quiz 26—C

Quiz 27—D

Quiz 28—C

Quiz 29—A

Quiz 30—B

ANSWERS

LEVEL 2

Quiz 1—C	Quiz 16—C
Quiz 2—D	Quiz 17—B
Quiz 3—B	Quiz 18—C
Quiz 4—B	Quiz 19—B
Quiz 5—A	Quiz 20—A
Quiz 6—C	Quiz 21—C
Quiz 7—B	Quiz 22—D
Quiz 8—D	Quiz 23—D
Quiz 9—A	Quiz 24—C
Quiz 10—D	Quiz 25—A
Quiz 11—A	Quiz 26—A
Quiz 12—C	Quiz 27—B
Quiz 13—D	Quiz 28—C
Quiz 14—C	Quiz 29—D
Quiz 15—B	Quiz 30—D

ANSWERS

LEVEL 3

Quiz 1—A
Quiz 2—B
Quiz 3—C
Quiz 4—C
Quiz 5—A
Quiz 6—D
Quiz 7—B
Quiz 8—C
Quiz 9—D
Quiz 10—C
Quiz 11—D
Quiz 12—B
Quiz 13—A
Quiz 14—A
Quiz 15—B

Quiz 16—D
Quiz 17—C
Quiz 18—A
Quiz 19—B
Quiz 20—A
Quiz 21—B
Quiz 22—C
Quiz 23—C
Quiz 24—B
Quiz 25—B
Quiz 26—A
Quiz 27—A
Quiz 28—C
Quiz 29—A
Quiz 30—D

ANSWERS

BIBLE BRONZE

Quiz 1—C	Quiz 16—C
Quiz 2—B	Quiz 17—A
Quiz 3—A	Quiz 18—C
Quiz 4—B	Quiz 19—D
Quiz 5—C	Quiz 20—C
Quiz 6—B	Quiz 21—D
Quiz 7—C	Quiz 22—B
Quiz 8—B	Quiz 23—A
Quiz 9—A	Quiz 24—B
Quiz 10—B	Quiz 25—C
Quiz 11—A	Quiz 26—B
Quiz 12—D	Quiz 27—B
Quiz 13—C	Quiz 28—A
Quiz 14—C	Quiz 29—D
Quiz 15—B	Quiz 30—A

ANSWERS

LEVEL 5

Quiz 1—A	Quiz 16—C
Quiz 2—A	Quiz 17—B
Quiz 3—B	Quiz 18—D
Quiz 4—D	Quiz 19—A
Quiz 5—A	Quiz 20—B
Quiz 6—C	Quiz 21—A
Quiz 7—B	Quiz 22—C
Quiz 8—B	Quiz 23—B
Quiz 9—A	Quiz 24—C
Quiz 10—C	Quiz 25—D
Quiz 11—D	Quiz 26—A
Quiz 12—A	Quiz 27—D
Quiz 13—D	Quiz 28—C
Quiz 14—B	Quiz 29—C
Quiz 15—D	Quiz 30—D

ANSWERS

LEVEL 6

Quiz 1—B	Quiz 16—C
Quiz 2—C	Quiz 17—C
Quiz 3—D	Quiz 18—A
Quiz 4—A	Quiz 19—B
Quiz 5—D	Quiz 20—D
Quiz 6—D	Quiz 21—A
Quiz 7—A	Quiz 22—C
Quiz 8—C	Quiz 23—B
Quiz 9—D	Quiz 24—B
Quiz 10—B	Quiz 25—A
Quiz 11—C	Quiz 26—D
Quiz 12—B	Quiz 27—A
Quiz 13—A	Quiz 28—A
Quiz 14—D	Quiz 29—D
Quiz 15—D	Quiz 30—B

ANSWERS

LEVEL 7

Quiz 1—C	Quiz 16—B
Quiz 2—D	Quiz 17—A
Quiz 3—A	Quiz 18—A
Quiz 4—D	Quiz 19—D
Quiz 5—B	Quiz 20—B
Quiz 6—C	Quiz 21—C
Quiz 7—A	Quiz 22—D
Quiz 8—B	Quiz 23—C
Quiz 9—B	Quiz 24—B
Quiz 10—A	Quiz 25—D
Quiz 11—C	Quiz 26—C
Quiz 12—A	Quiz 27—B
Quiz 13—C	Quiz 28—A
Quiz 14—C	Quiz 29—D
Quiz 15—B	Quiz 30—A

ANSWERS

BIBLE SILVER

Quiz 1—A
Quiz 2—B
Quiz 3—D
Quiz 4—A
Quiz 5—A
Quiz 6—B
Quiz 7—C
Quiz 8—C
Quiz 9—A
Quiz 10—C
Quiz 11—D
Quiz 12—A
Quiz 13—A
Quiz 14—C
Quiz 15—B

Quiz 16—D
Quiz 17—C
Quiz 18—B
Quiz 19—B
Quiz 20—A
Quiz 21—C
Quiz 22—B
Quiz 23—D
Quiz 24—C
Quiz 25—A
Quiz 26—D
Quiz 27—C
Quiz 28—C
Quiz 29—B
Quiz 30—B

ANSWERS

LEVEL 9

Quiz 1—C	Quiz 16—A
Quiz 2—B	Quiz 17—A
Quiz 3—C	Quiz 18—C
Quiz 4—D	Quiz 19—A
Quiz 5—D	Quiz 20—D
Quiz 6—A	Quiz 21—B
Quiz 7—A	Quiz 22—B
Quiz 8—C	Quiz 23—D
Quiz 9—D	Quiz 24—C
Quiz 10—C	Quiz 25—B
Quiz 11—C	Quiz 26—A
Quiz 12—A	Quiz 27—B
Quiz 13—C	Quiz 28—C
Quiz 14—B	Quiz 29—C
Quiz 15—C	Quiz 30—D

ANSWERS

LEVEL 10

Quiz 1—A
Quiz 2—D
Quiz 3—B
Quiz 4—B
Quiz 5—C
Quiz 6—C
Quiz 7—B
Quiz 8—D
Quiz 9—C
Quiz 10—B
Quiz 11—A
Quiz 12—C
Quiz 13—D
Quiz 14—A
Quiz 15—B

Quiz 16—C
Quiz 17—D
Quiz 18—C
Quiz 19—B
Quiz 20—A
Quiz 21—D
Quiz 22—D
Quiz 23—B
Quiz 24—A
Quiz 25—C
Quiz 26—D
Quiz 27—B
Quiz 28—A
Quiz 29—D
Quiz 30—A

ANSWERS

LEVEL 11

Quiz 1—D	Quiz 16—C
Quiz 2—B	Quiz 17—A
Quiz 3—B	Quiz 18—C
Quiz 4—A	Quiz 19—C
Quiz 5—C	Quiz 20—A
Quiz 6—A	Quiz 21—D
Quiz 7—D	Quiz 22—C
Quiz 8—A	Quiz 23—C
Quiz 9—B	Quiz 24—D
Quiz 10—D	Quiz 25—D
Quiz 11—B	Quiz 26—C
Quiz 12—A	Quiz 27—A
Quiz 13—A	Quiz 28—C
Quiz 14—C	Quiz 29—D
Quiz 15—D	Quiz 30—C

ANSWERS

BIBLE GOLD

Quiz 1—C	Quiz 16—B
Quiz 2—D	Quiz 17—A
Quiz 3—A	Quiz 18—B
Quiz 4—B	Quiz 19—A
Quiz 5—C	Quiz 20—D
Quiz 6—C	Quiz 21—B
Quiz 7—A	Quiz 22—D
Quiz 8—B	Quiz 23—A
Quiz 9—A	Quiz 24—A
Quiz 10—D	Quiz 25—C
Quiz 11—B	Quiz 26—B
Quiz 12—D	Quiz 27—B
Quiz 13—D	Quiz 28—C
Quiz 14—D	Quiz 29—B
Quiz 15—C	Quiz 30—D

LIKE BIBLE TRIVIA?

Then check out these great books from Barbour Publishing!

The Bible Detective by Carol Smith
Solve mysteries posed by a mixed-up story using biblical characters, places, and quotations.
ISBN 1-57748-838-5/Paperback/224 pages/$2.97

My Final Answer by Paul Kent
Thirty separate quizzes feature twelve multiple-choice questions each—and the questions get progressively harder!
ISBN 1-58660-030-3/Paperback/256 pages/$2.97

Bible IQ by Rayburn Ray
One hundred sections of ten questions each—and a systematic scoring system to tell you just how well you did.
ISBN 1-57748-837-7/Paperback/256 pages/$2.97

Test Your Bible Knowledge by Carl Shoup
Over 1,400 multiple-choice questions to test your mettle, tickle your funny bone, and tantalize your intellect.
ISBN 1-55748-541-0/Paperback/224 pages/$2.97

Fun Facts About the Bible by Robyn Martins
Challenging and intriguing Bible trivia—expect some of the answers to surprise you!
ISBN 1-55748-897-5/Paperback/256 pages/$2.97

Available wherever books are sold.
Or order from:

Barbour Publishing, Inc.
P.O. Box 719
Uhrichsville, OH 44683
http://www.barbourbooks.com

If you order by mail add $2.00 to your order for shipping.
Prices subject to change without notice.